VICTORY HALL PRESS

VICTORY HALL YEARBOOK

DRAWING ROOMS | 926 NEWARK AVE, JERSEY CITY

Drawing Rooms is operated by Victory Hall Inc. a 501c3 non-profit organization producing exhibitions, programs and public art projects in the NJ/NY area since 2001. Victory Hall Inc. programs include Rainbow Thursdays Artists (art classes for developmentally disabled adults), Victory Hall Press and The Art Project, exhibition development for Art House, The Oakman and Hamilton House.

YEARBOOK PRODUCTION:
Interior Design/Layout: Alejandro Rubin
Editors: James Pustorino, Anne Trauben
Cover Design: James Pustorino

Victory Hall Press
926 Newark Ave
Jersey City, NJ 07306
December 2018
ISBN: 9781790490356

This program is made possible in part by funds from the New Jersey State Council on the Arts/Department of State, a partner agency of the National Endowment for the Arts, administered by the Hudson County Office of Cultural and Heritage Affairs, Thomas A. DeGise, County Executive, and the Board of Chosen Freeholders.

Table of Contents

Victory Hall Yearbook Introduction 4

Our Move 6

2018 Holiday Fundraiser Catalogue 8

Drawing Rooms Exhibitions 14

    The Big Small Show

    Somewhere Over the Interconnected Rainbow and Prospero's Grand St. Masque

    Now Ya See it Now Ya Don't / Open and Shut / Sneak Peak / Not Ready for Prime Time / This is Not the Grand Opening: Drawing Rooms Presents The Artists of the Topps Building

The Art Project 33

    Noyes Museum, Drawing Rooms Art Project: JC in AC

    109 Columbus Ave

    The Oakman

    The Art House

    Hamilton House

Rainbow Thursdays Artists 44

    Sunflower Adult Medical Day Care Center

    Windmill Center

DRAWING ROOMS 2018: What We Did On Our Summer Vacation

When the new year started, we didn't know that we would spend the summer building a new art space for Drawing Rooms, but that is what we did. Our gallery in the Topps building redefines us as an arts space. For the first time, we have our own space to grow in and we are very excited about our future.

The following pages chronicle the story of what our non-profit, Victory Hall Inc. did all this year, especially during the spring and summer months when the future of our organization occupied so much of our time and energy.

It all started in early Spring 2018, when we found out that we needed to leave the convent building on Grand Street in Downtown Jersey City where our arts center had been since 2012. We had to move quickly to figure out what kind of space we wanted, we where we should go, and of course, how we would pay for it. So although it wasn't what we had planned, we were able to figure out our next steps and we like where we are heading now. And in the process, we were also able to accomplish a lot.

Drawing Rooms began 2018 at our 180 Grand St. Jersey City location with The Big Small Show, featuring over 100 artists from New Jersey, New York and Connecticut. Then, in March, after learning of the building decision, we spent a couple of months searching and planning for our new location. In April, we produced an exhibition with Noyes Museum in the Noyes Art Garage in Atlantic City and then in May, we planned the last show at our ten-room convent exhibition space. Somewhere Over the Interconnected Rainbow/Prospero's Grand St Masque was to be both the closing exhibition and event, borrowing its concept from the famous last party of Edgar Allan Poe's Masque of Red Death, making use of our multiple rooms, each featuring a different color. Over 175 artists came together from our own community and from as far away as Scotland and France, to donate works for

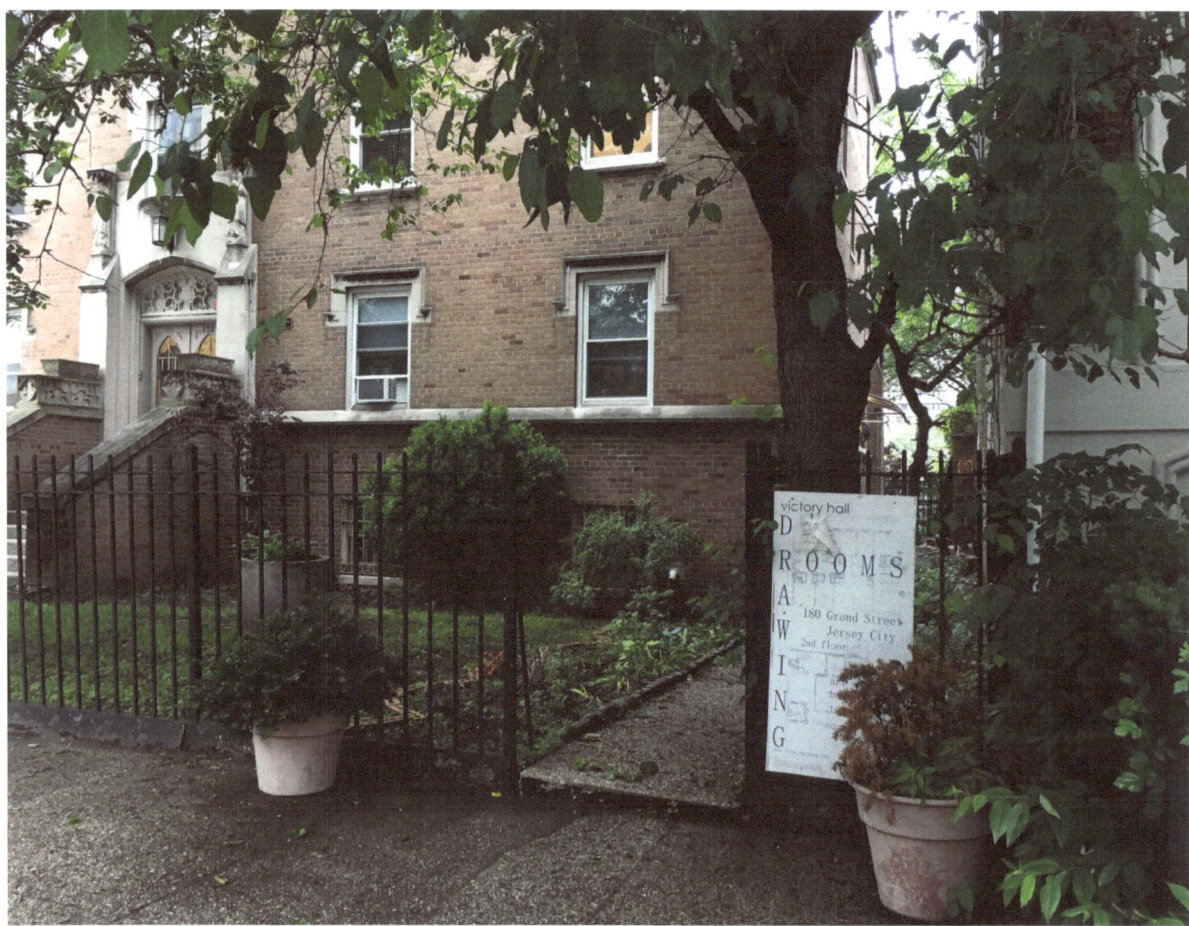

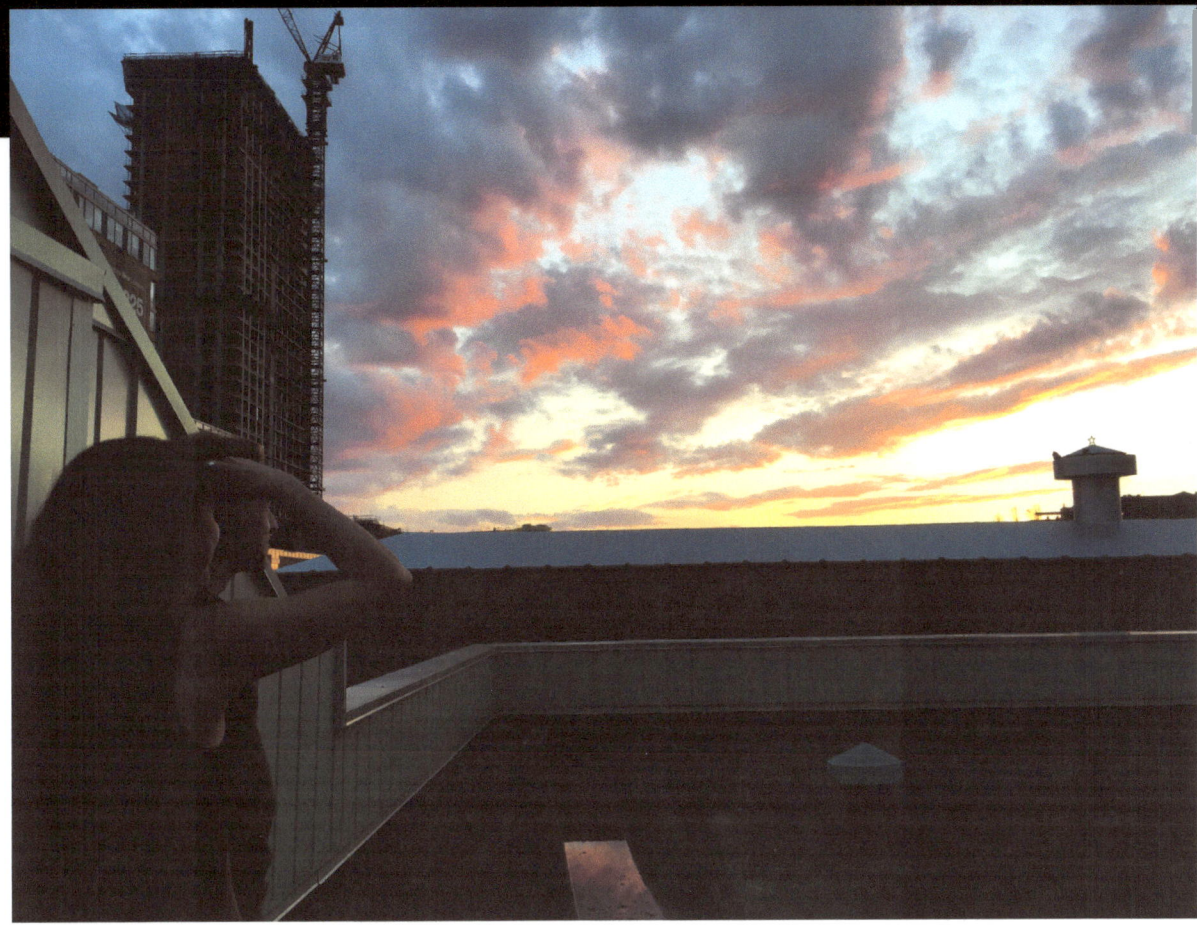

this final fundraiser. This support was a great encouragement and was only the beginning. So many people bought works and made monetary donations. From this flow of support, along with extra help from trusted funders, such as the Geraldine R. Dodge Foundation, we were able to confidently move ahead with planning and construction on our new exhibit space.

While construction was happening at the new Drawing Rooms, summer was a time of launching many off-site exhibits. The Art Project, our exhibit program in the lobbies of Shuster Management's Jersey City buildings, began in June with a two-artist exhibit at Gallery 109 Columbus, followed by 40 solo-artist lobby exhibits between August and October. The project creates opportunities for many area artists to display a small body of their work, and also features ongoing tours of the lobbies.

Rainbow Thursdays Artists, our program for developmentally disabled adults, had been running weekly all year, and their summer exhibit at the Bayonne Public Library focused on July 4th themes: the Statue of Liberty, fireworks and celebration.

In fall, we felt we were ready to open the doors at the new space and give the public a glimpse of what we had been working on all summer. The 'Now Ya See It ...' exhibit for Jersey City Artists Studio Tour gathered artists who have studios in the Topps Building, our new location, along with work from the artists of Drawing Rooms. Opening our space begins a new relationship with the Journal Square neighborhood and with our next-door neighbor, Mana Contemporary, introducing Drawing Rooms to a new audience, while we welcome back many of those who have been with us all along the way, artists and art-goers alike.

The combined community support enables us to meet the challenges of creating the best possible situations and venues we can for as many artists to show their work and for as many people to view it. Bringing art into the lives of the community around us and making a place for artists to thrive in our community.

As we look forward to the New year, and make plans for what Drawing Rooms will be, we are grateful to all those appreciated who we have been and all we have done and all who joined with us in this year's efforts.

James Pustorino & Anne Trauben

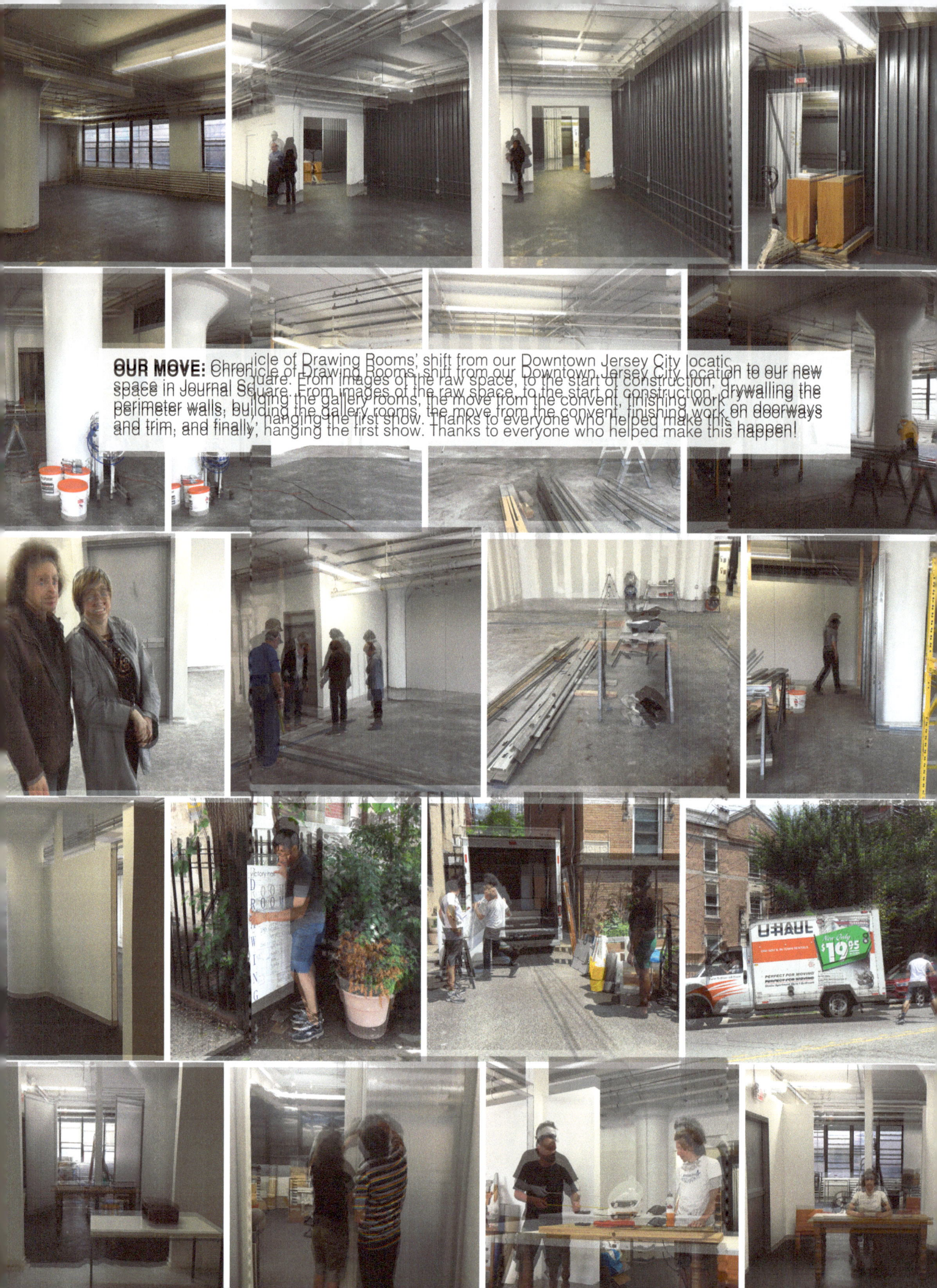

OUR MOVE: Chronicle of Drawing Rooms' shift from our Downtown Jersey City location to our new space in Journal Square. From images of the raw space, to the start of construction, drywalling the perimeter walls, building the gallery rooms, the move from the convent, finishing work on doorways and trim, and finally, hanging the first show. Thanks to everyone who helped make this happen!

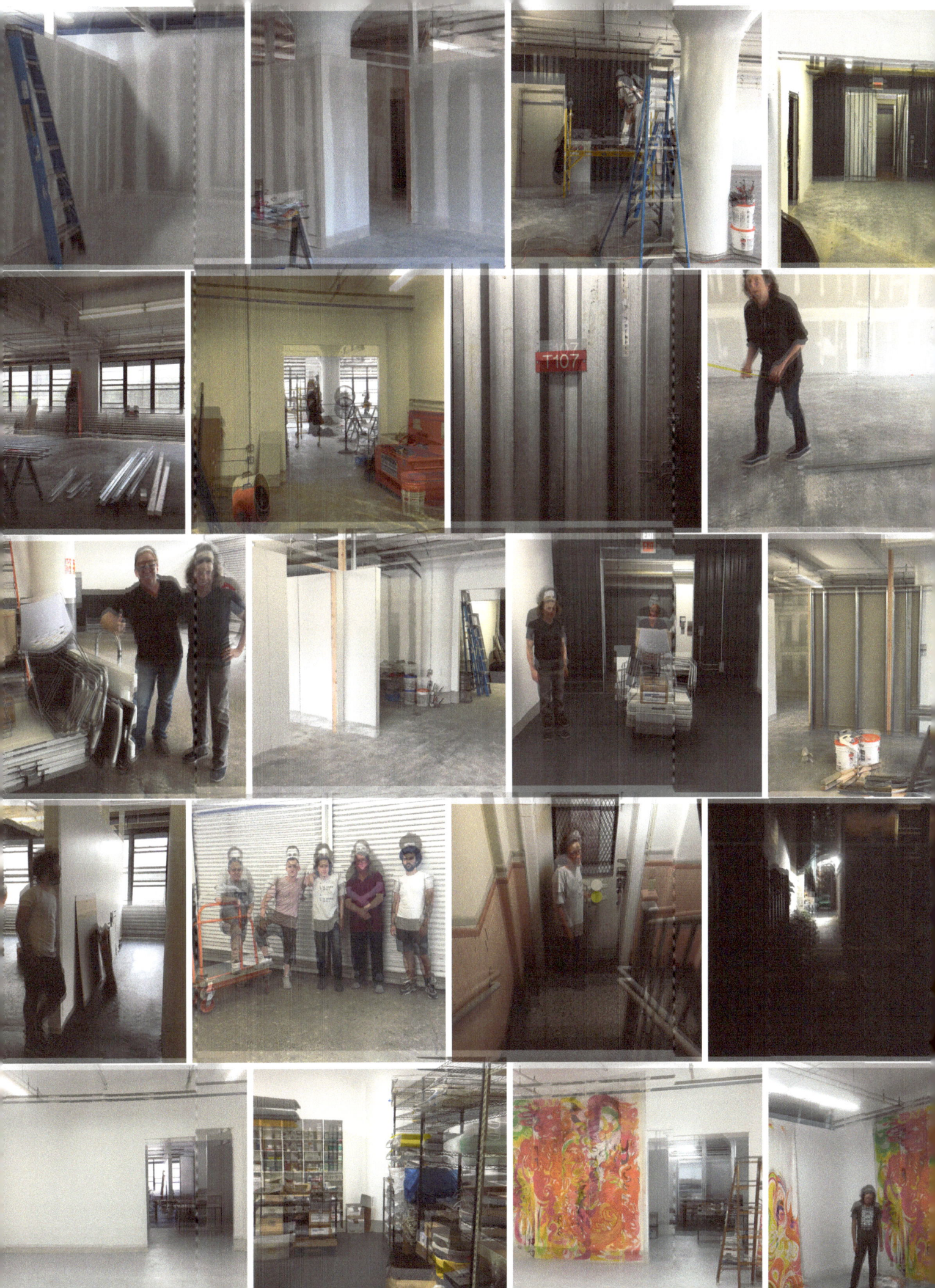

Holiday Fundraiser

Dawing Rooms Holiday Fundraiser:
"Take Home a Work of Art"

Thursday, December 6, 2018, 7-9p

DRAWING ROOMS
926 Newark Ave, # T107
Jersey City, NJ

Help Us To Continue Providing Excellent Programming in Our Unique Space and BRING HOME A FAVORITE ARTIST'S WORK!

Artists have generously donated original drawings, paintings and sculpture in support of our 6th Holiday Fundraiser, celebrating our 6th year of exhibitions and community programming! The Fundraiser Evening includes wine, hors d'oeuvres from fine restaurants, music, and a raffle of donated artworks. Ticket Prices ensures you a Work of Art of your choice!

Here's How It Works: Artwork will be selected on the fundraiser evening by a raffle drawing, which determines the order in which primary ticket holders make their selection. With a little bit of luck in the drawing, you can go home with a piece worth several times more than the cost of a ticket. Thanks to all the artists who donated works this year!

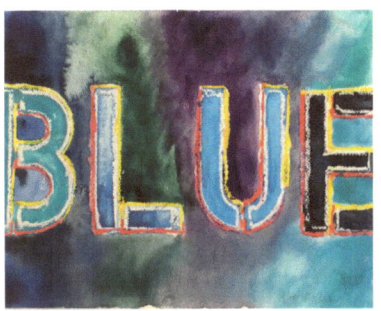
Alan Walker

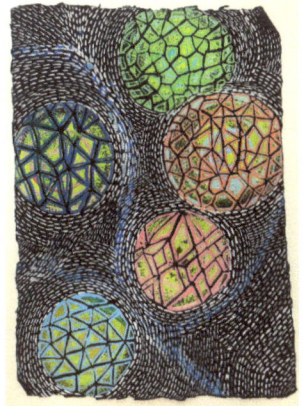
Alexi Brock

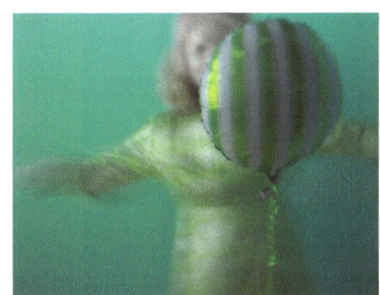
Aleya Lehmann

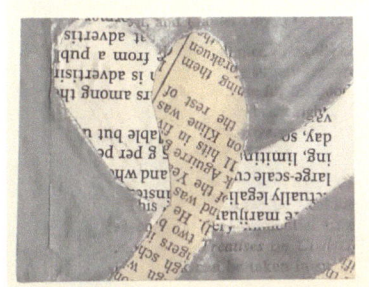
Amy Basin

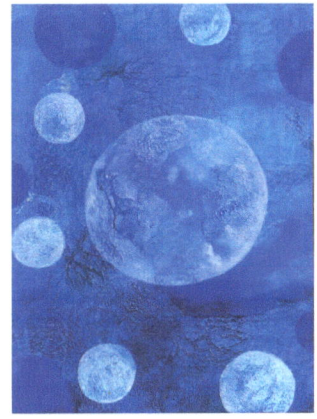
Andra Samelson

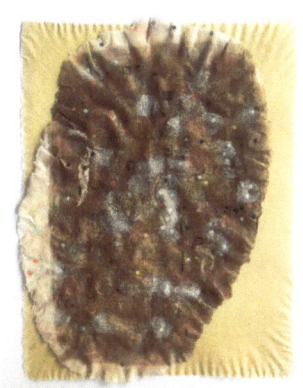
Anne McKeown

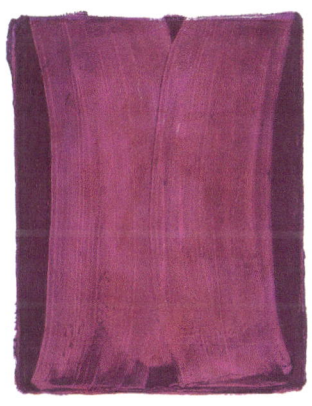
Anne Russinof

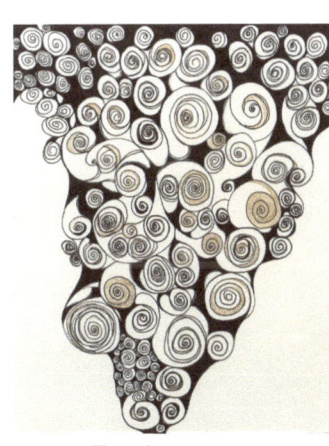
Anne Trauben

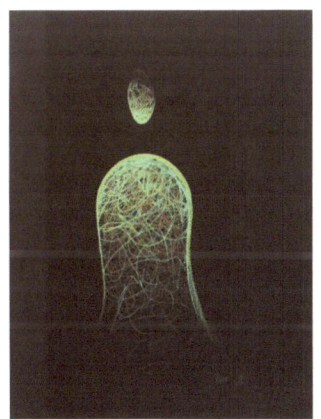
Bill Stamos

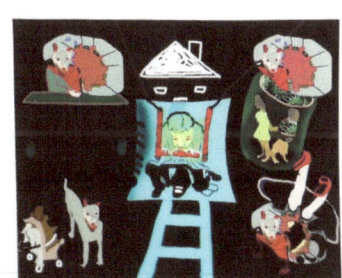
Carol Radsprecher

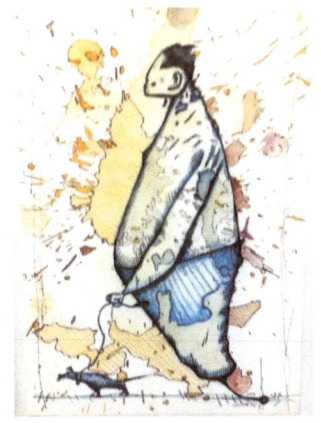
Cheryl Gross

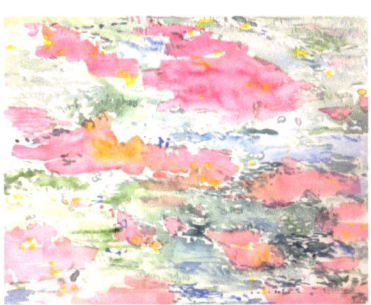
Claire McConaughy

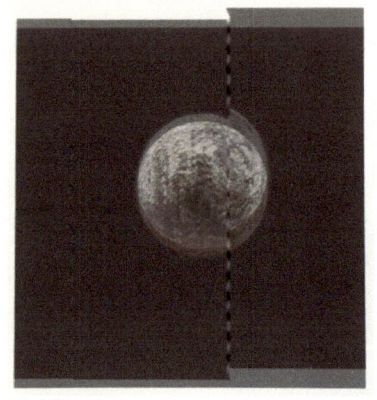
Ed Fausty

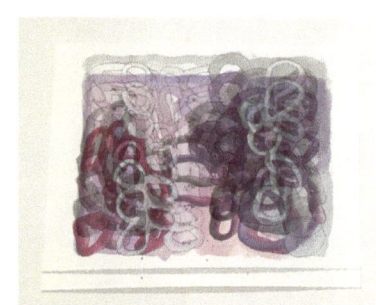
Elizabeth Onorato

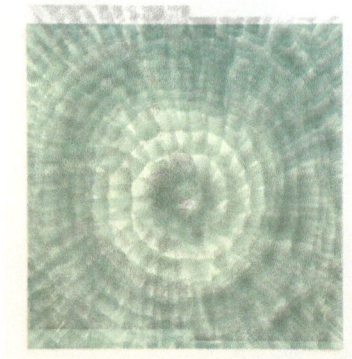
Ellie Murphy

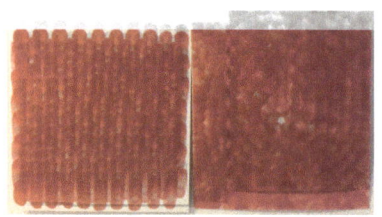
Ellie Murphy

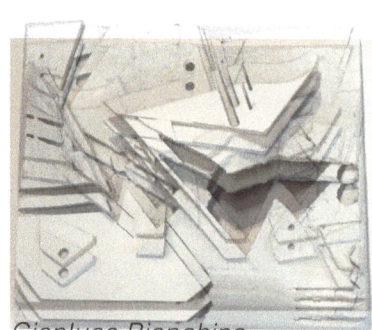
Gianluca Bianchino

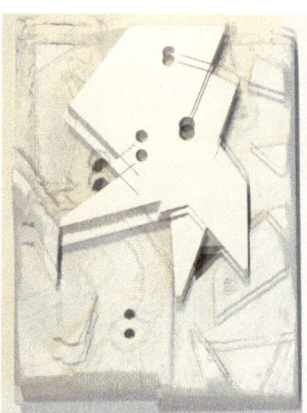
Gianluca Bianchino

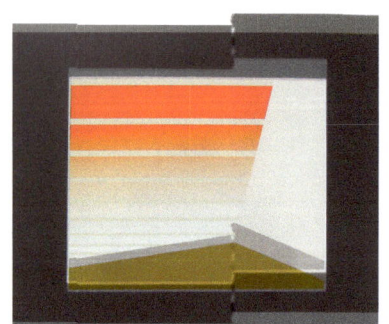
Greg Letson

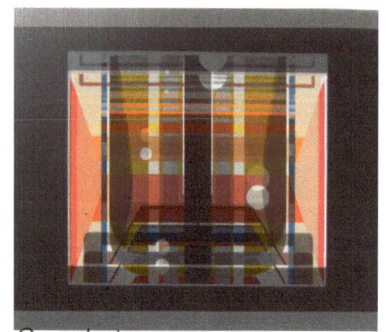
Greg Letson

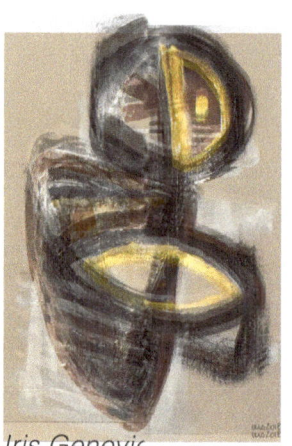
Iris Genevieve Lahens

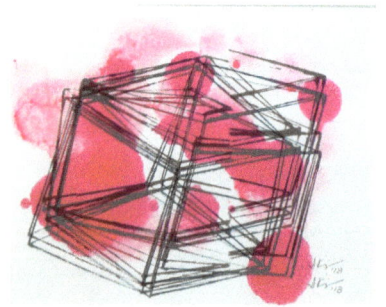
Iris Kufert-Rivo

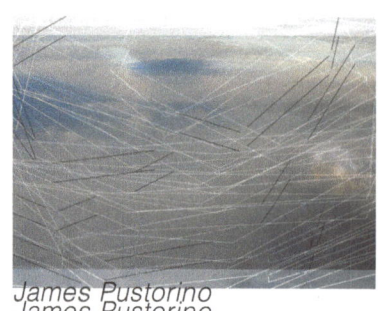
James Pustorino

James Pustorino

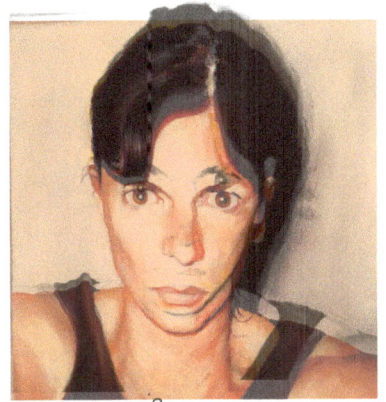
Janet Tsakis

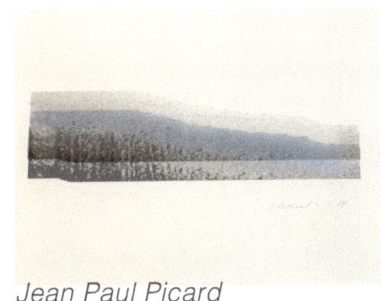
Jean Paul Picard

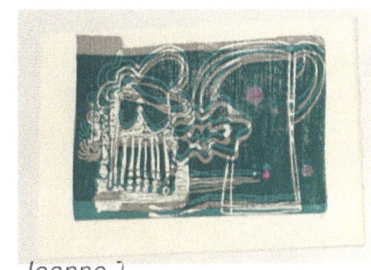
Jeanne Tremel

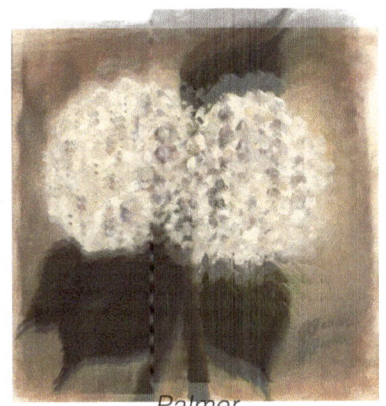
Joan Marie Palmer

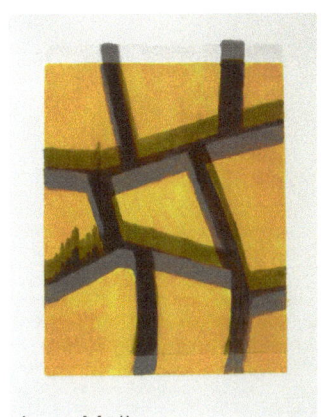
Joan Mellon

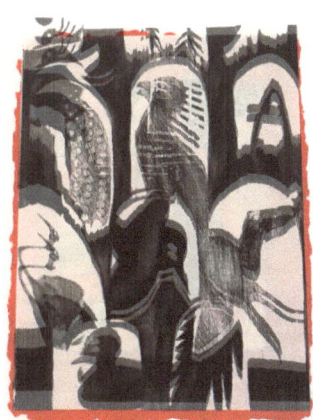
Jodi Fink

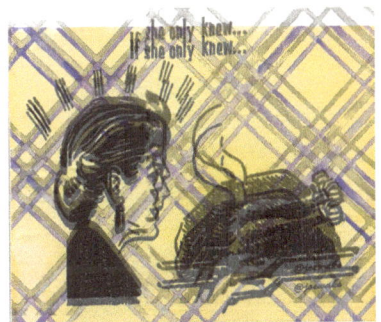
Joe Waks

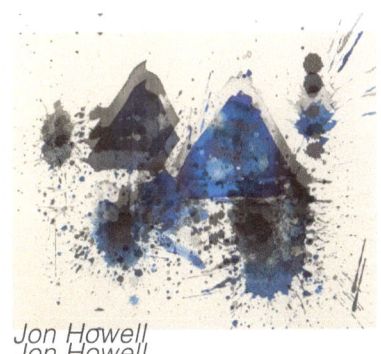
Jon Howell

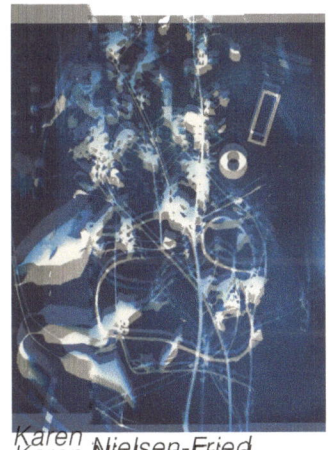
Karen Nielsen-Fried

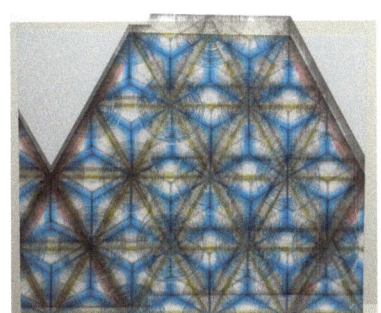
Kellie Murphy

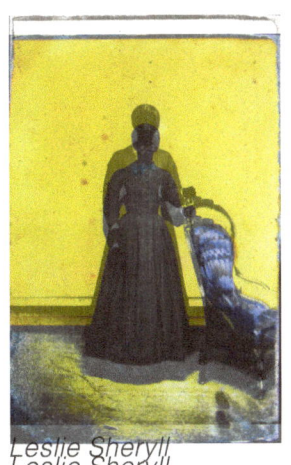
Leslie Sheryll

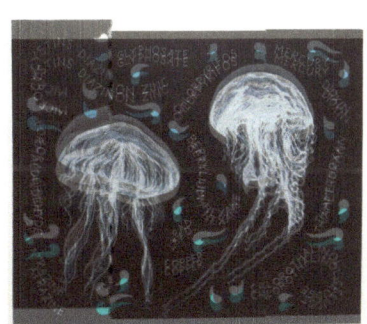
Linda Byrne

11 Holiday Fundraiser

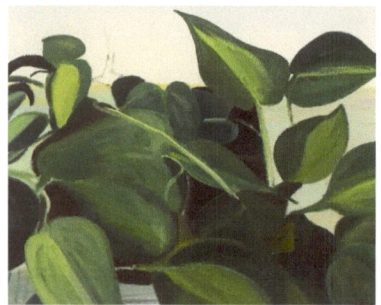
Linda Gottesfeld

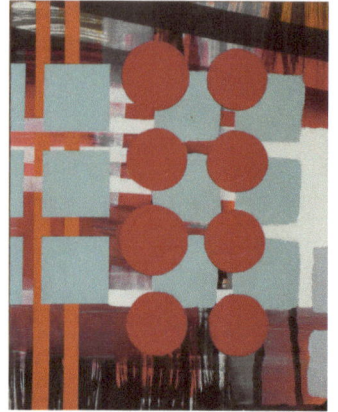
Linda Schmidt

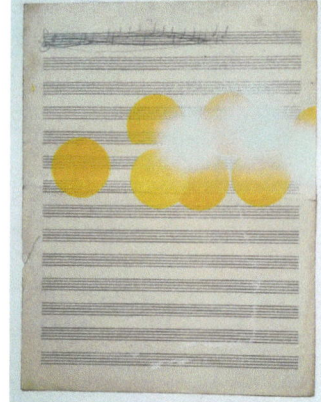
Michael Ensminger

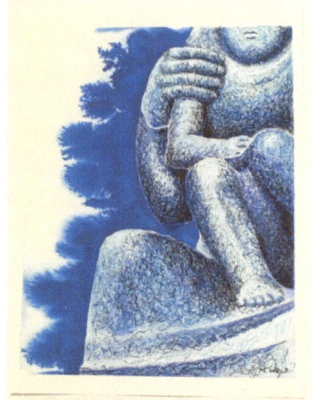
Michael Wolfe

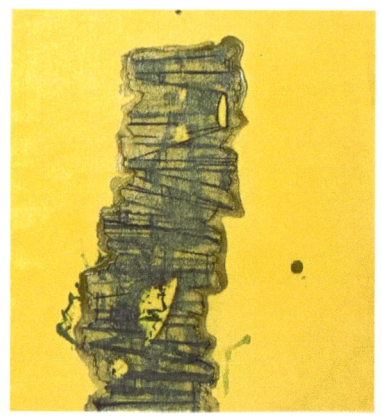
Michelle Mackey

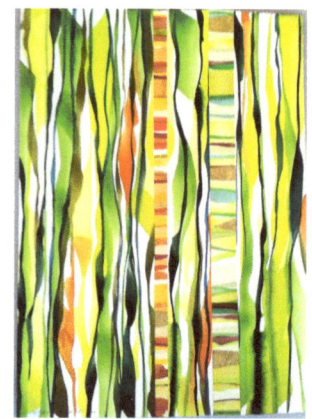
Mollie Thonneson

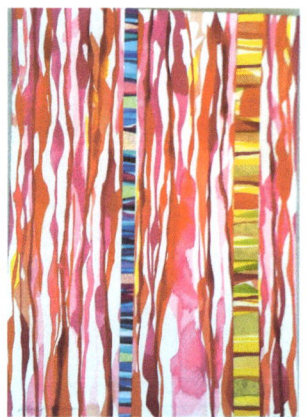
Mollie Thonneson

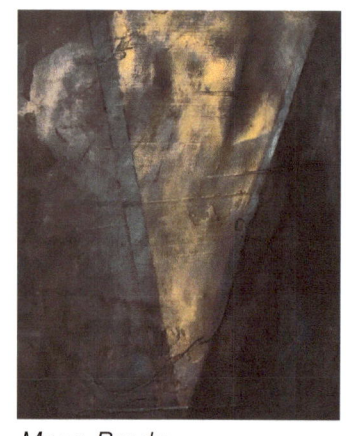
Mona Brody

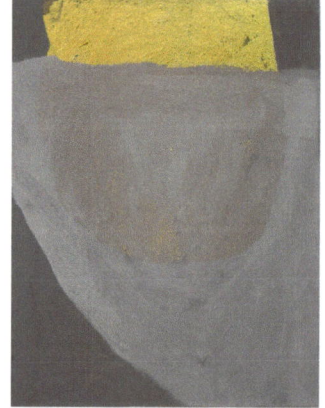
Mona Brody

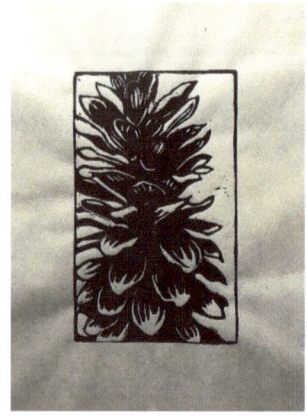
Nan Ring

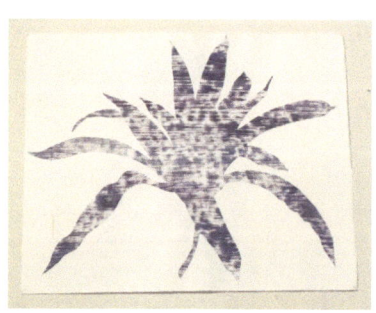
Nikolina Kovalenko

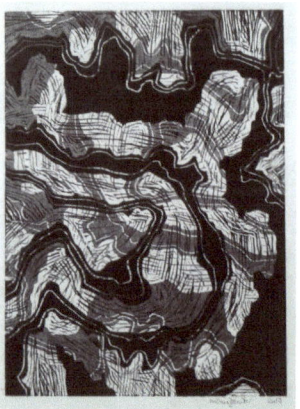
Noémie Jennifer

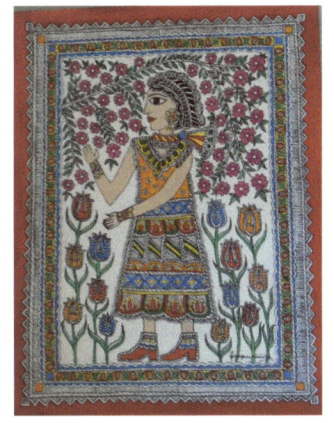
Nupur Nishith

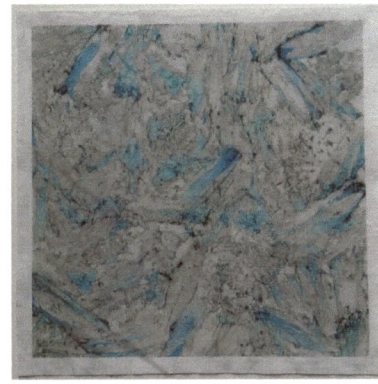
Pamela Shipley

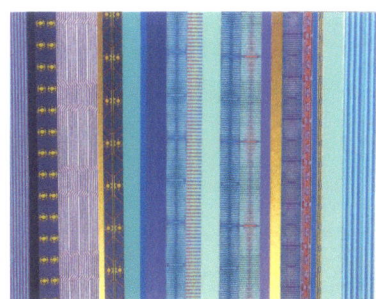
Pat Lay

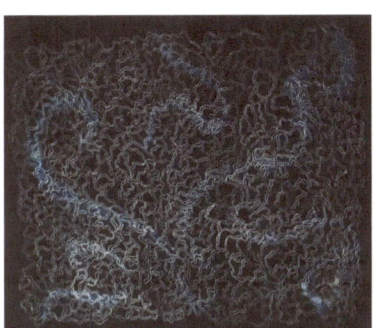
Robin Ellenbogen

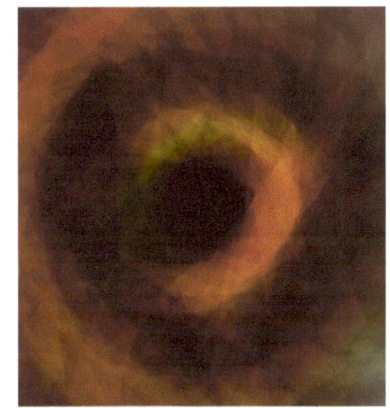
Roger Sayre

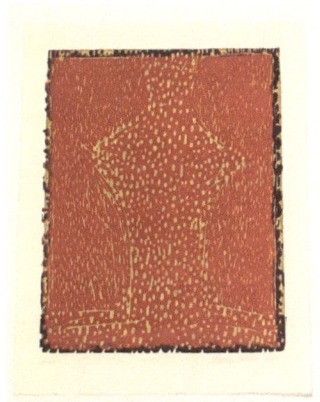
Shelly Haven

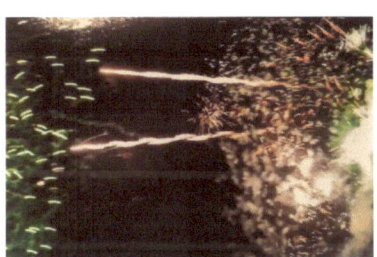
Stephen Krasner

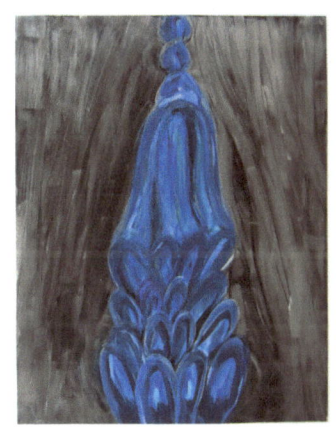
Theresa DeSalvio

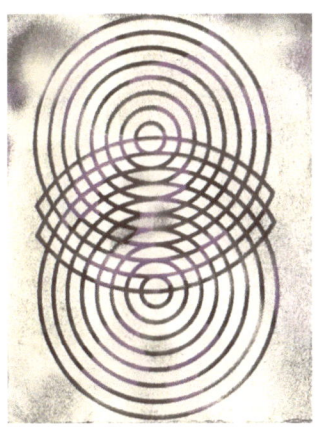
Wendy Letven

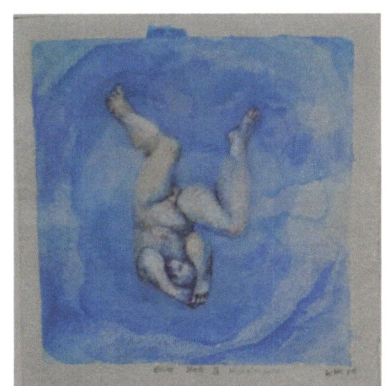
Winifred McNeil

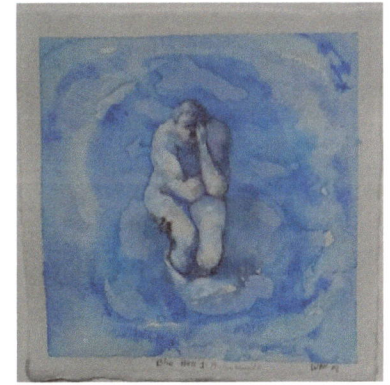
Winifred McNeil

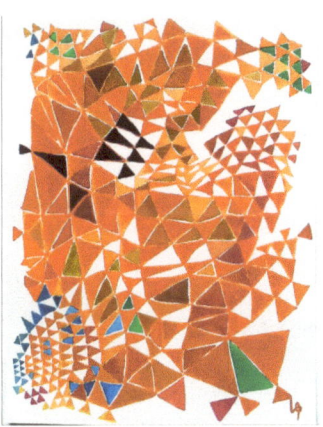
Yuko Nishakawa

13 Holiday Fundraiser

Drawing Rooms
Exhibitions

Drawing Rooms moved to the Topps Building in Journal Square in July 2018!

Drawing Rooms is our non-profit art space in the Topps Building in the Journal Square neighborhood in Jersey City. We recently moved from a former convent in Downtown Jersey City where we were for 5 years. We show two and three-dimensional works by emerging and mid-career artists in NJ and the NJ metropolitan area. We provide a place where artists can gather, connect and advance their careers. Our innovative and exciting exhibitions, public programs and publications enrich the lives of our community through an appreciation of and involvement with contemporary art.

Curator Anne Trauben works throughout the year visiting open studios, exhibitions and meeting artists from across New Jersey and the NYC area to bring together our Drawing Rooms gallery season.

The Big Small Show

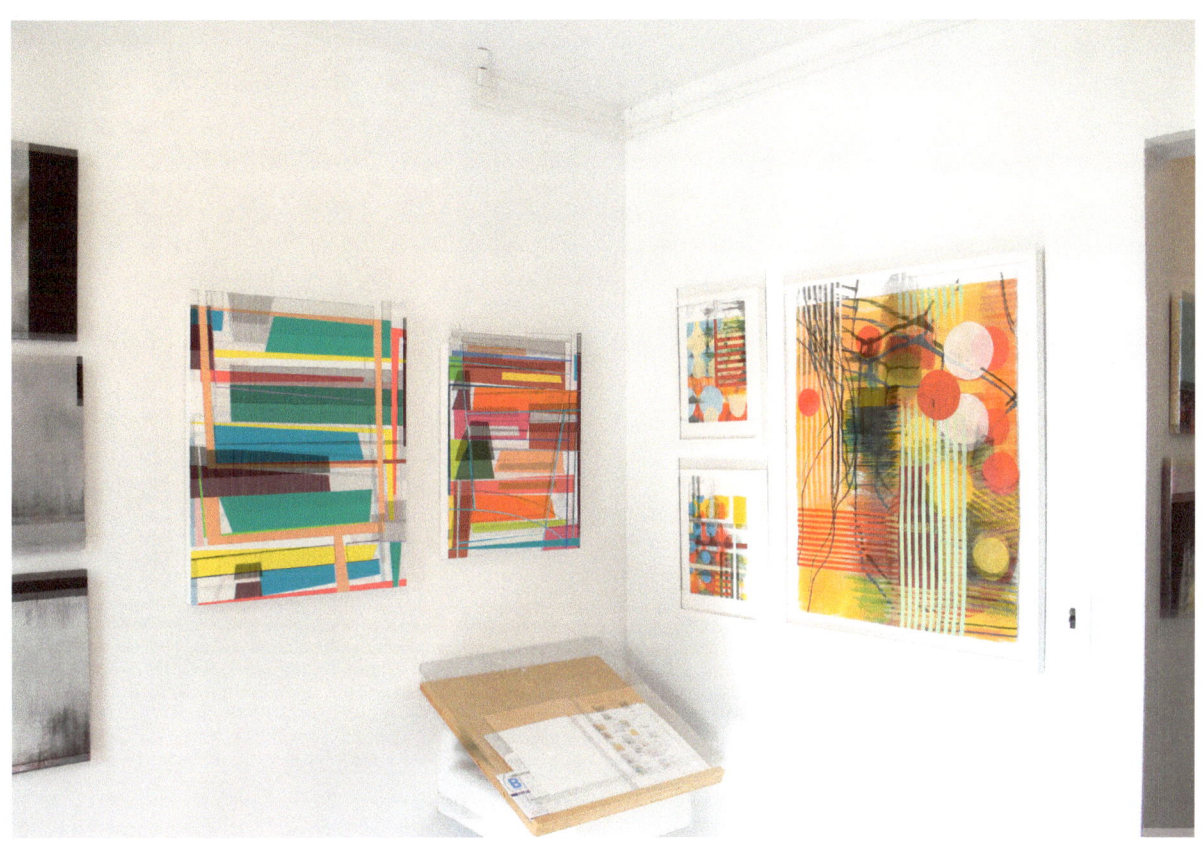

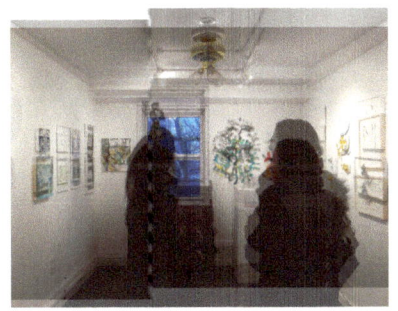
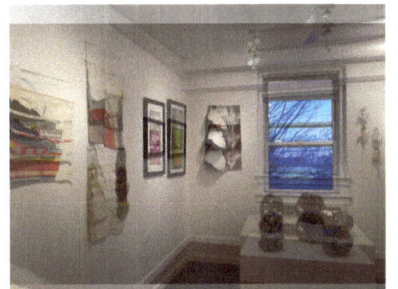
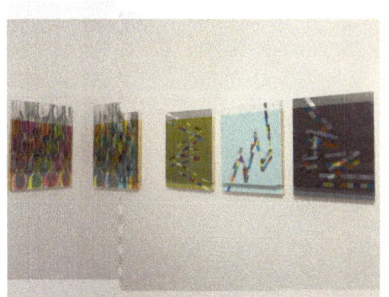
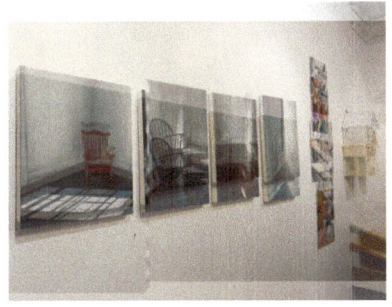
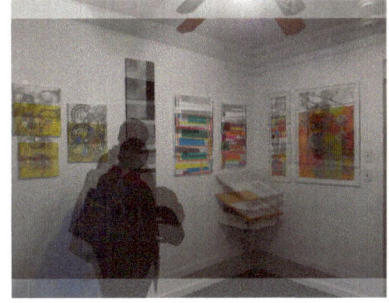
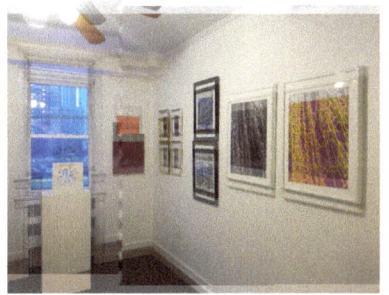

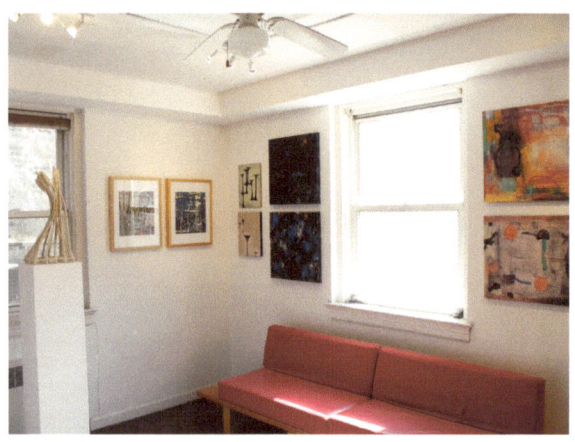
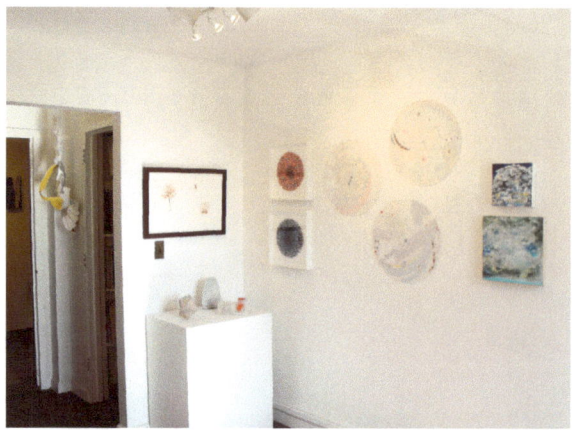
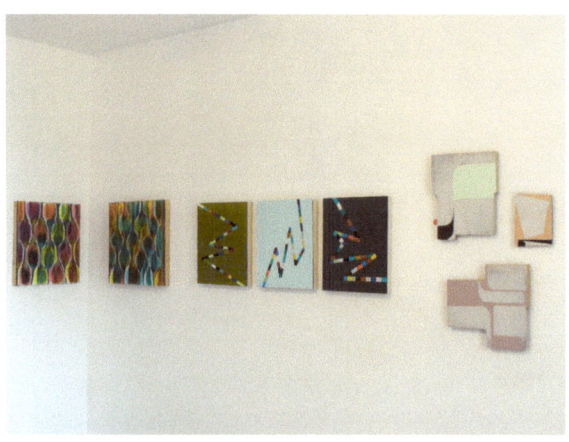
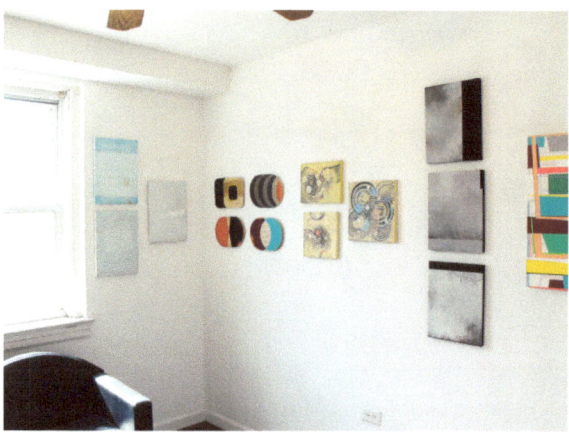
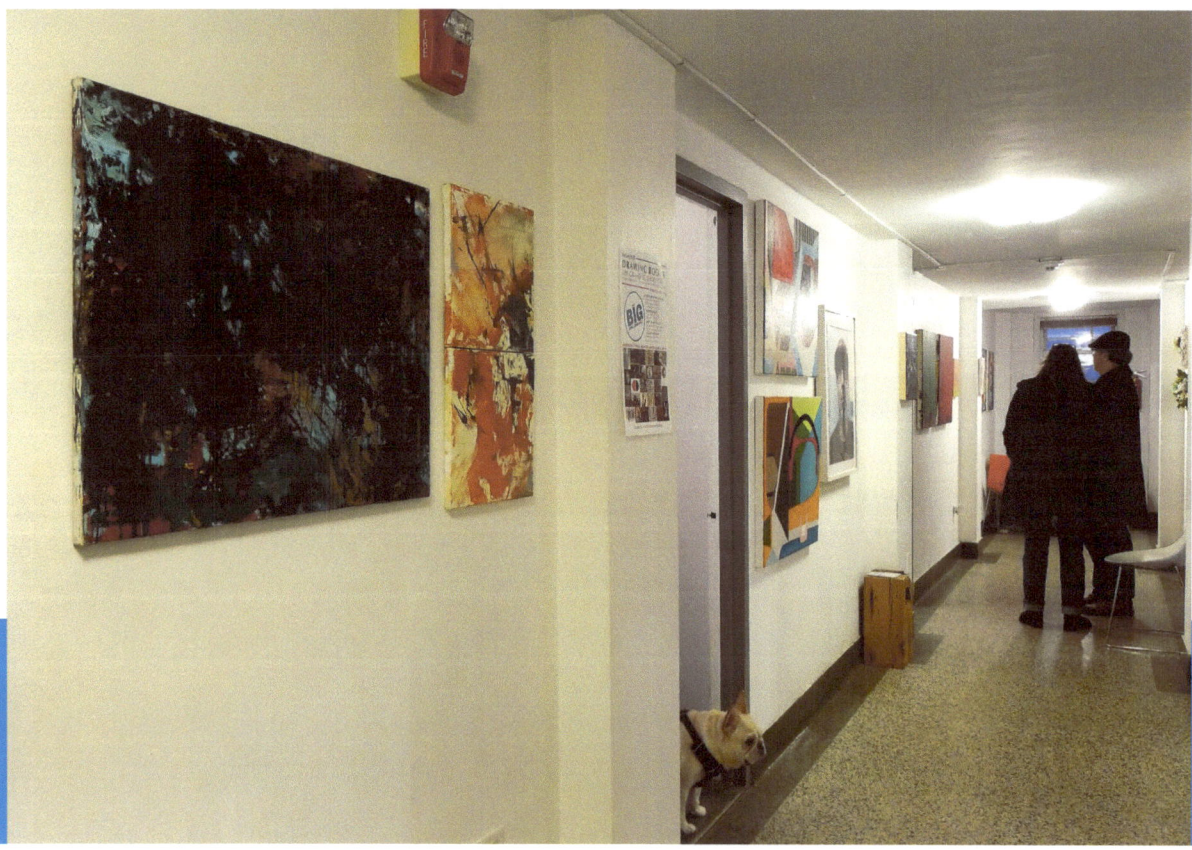

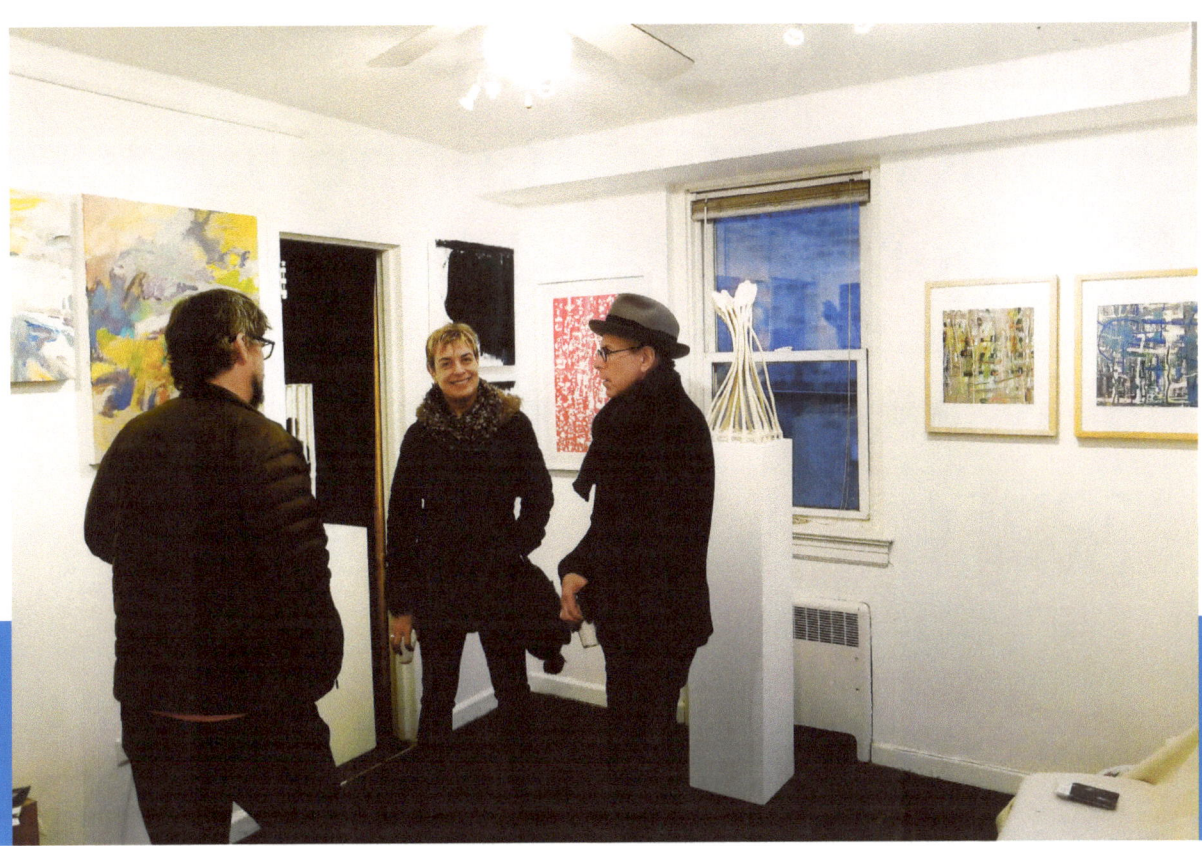

The Big Small Show
January 12th to Frebruary 17th, 2018

Our fifth annual small works show at Drawing Rooms, which ran from January 12, 2018 through Saturday, February 17, 2018, after the December 15-17 2017 opening weekend.

The sprawling exhibition brought together a large array of innovative and exceptional new works by over 100 artists from across New Jersey and the NY metropolitan area, allowing visitors to discover artists new to them. The intimate setting of multiple rooms in our converted convent created a place where art and artists connected with the public and with one another.

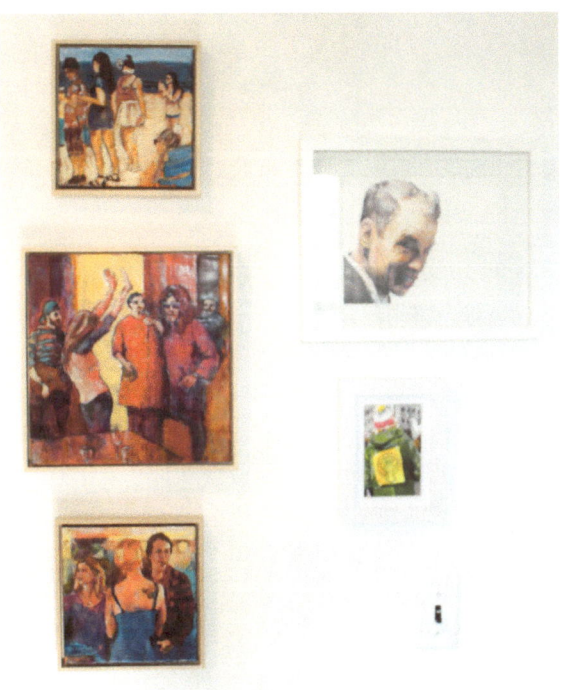

Somewhere Over the Interconnected Rainbow and Prospero's Grand St. Masque

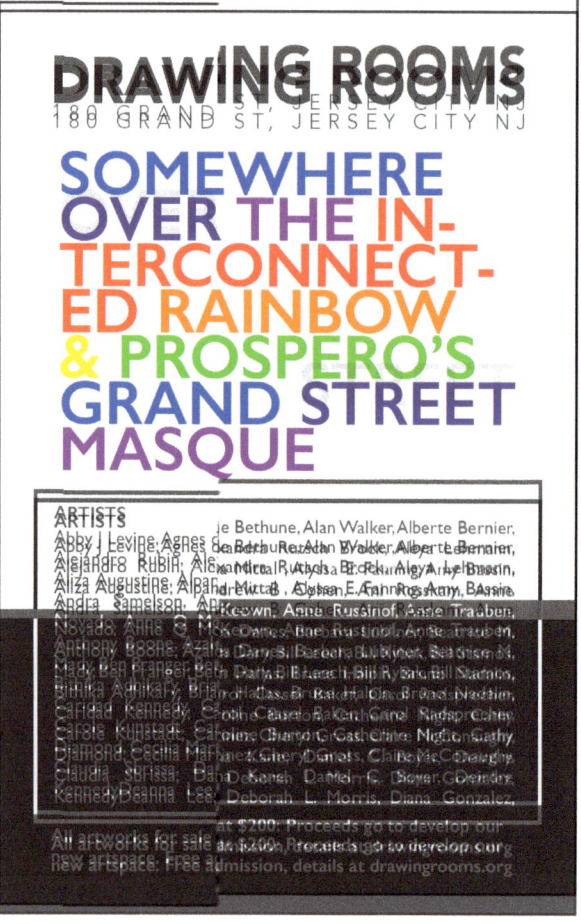

Somewhere Over the Interconnected Rainbow and Prospero's Grand St. Masque
Saturday 6/9/18 – Sunday 6/10/18

After five years of inventive exhibitions, Drawing Rooms needed to move from its current art space at the former convent building at 180 Grand St because the building was going to be repurposed. Drawing Rooms would be relocating to Topps Building at the Mana campus in Journal Square, and reinventing ourselves in a new gallery to continue our innovative programming. To celebrate the move, the downtown art space threw a final exhibition and fundraiser party on June 9th and June 10th. Both events were free and open to the public.

"The Topps Building is a storage building so we need to convert it into a gallery space," said James Pustorino, Director of Drawing Rooms. "We made the show a fundraiser to help out with costs of building the new gallery and moving in. We are excited to move to the Mana Campus because it's a hub for artistic activity in Jersey City."

Victory Hall started in 2001 in the Elks Club Hall when the OLC Church in Downtown Jersey City decided that it should be used as a community and cultural center. In 2012, Drawing Rooms began in the adjacent former convent. Although the building was old and had several maintenance issues, it ultimately served its purpose.

"The convent building had its advantages," said Pustorino. "We were able to repurpose the little rooms that the nuns from OLC used, as

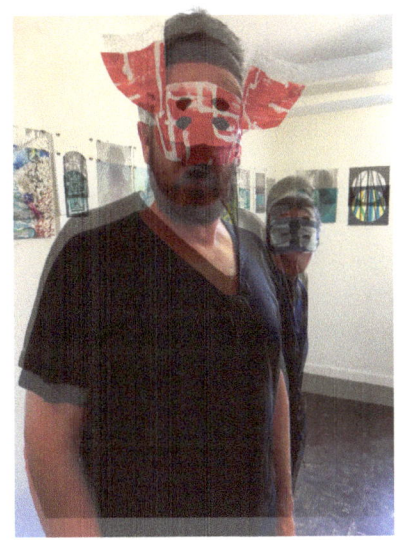
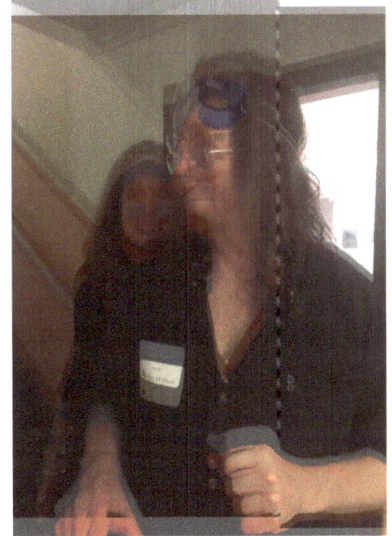
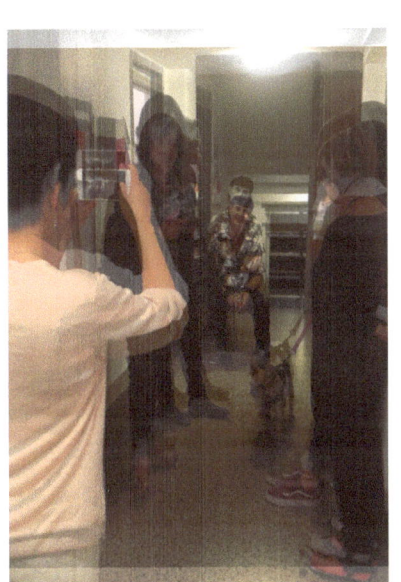
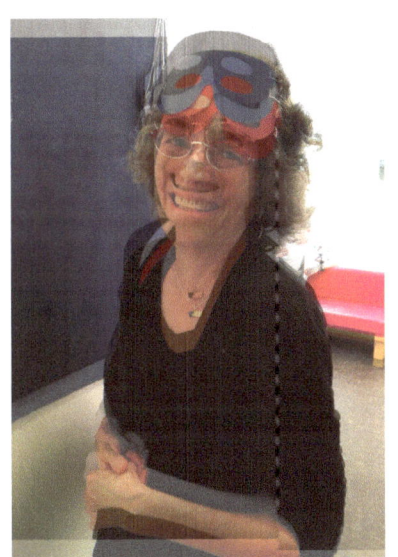
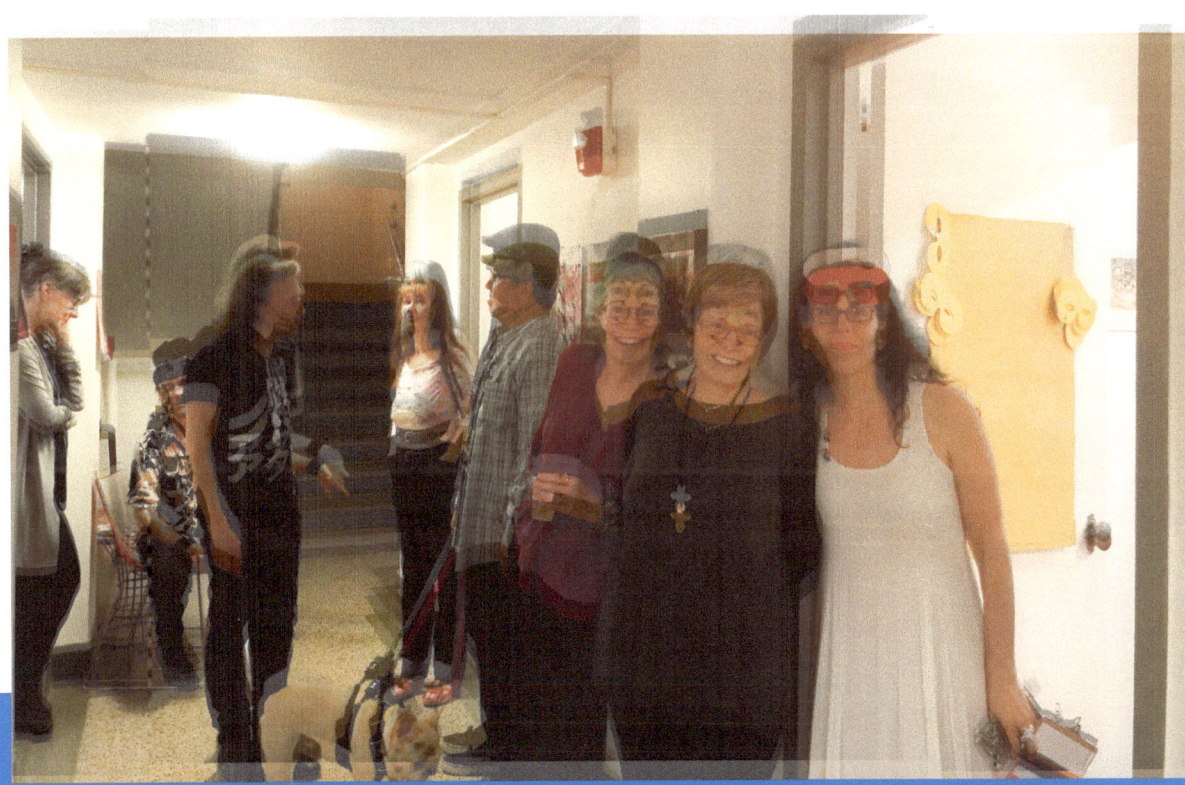

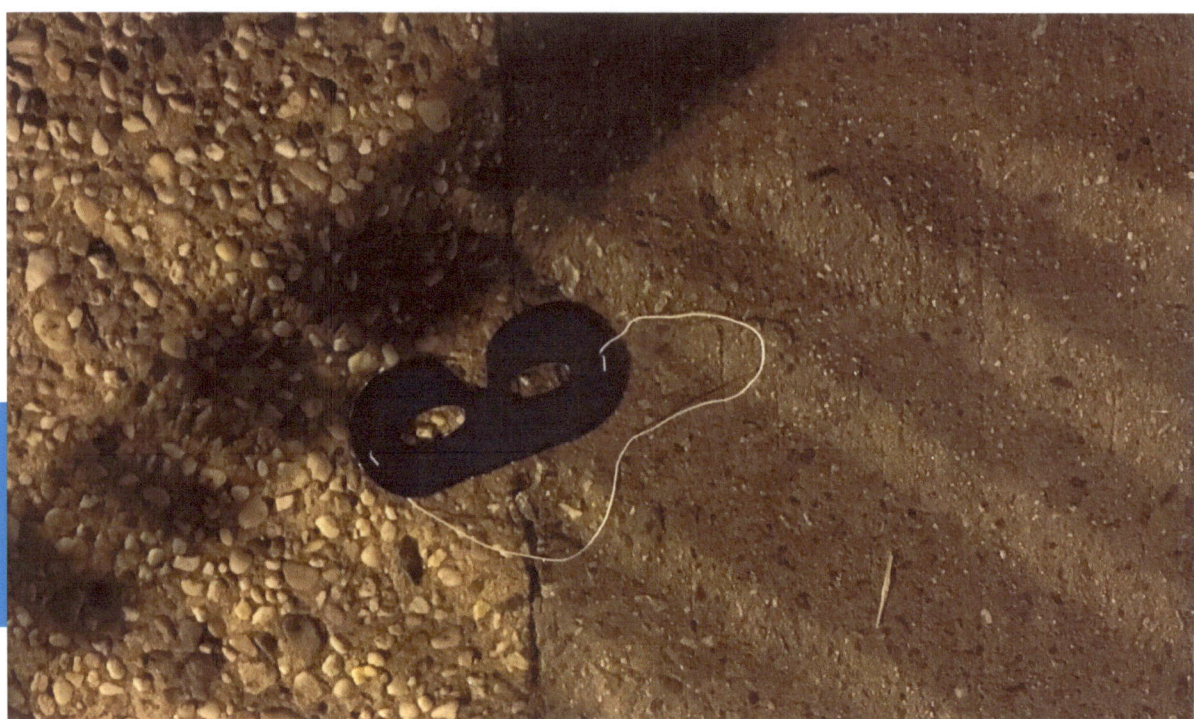

individual galleries. It was a great experience, but we're moving on, and this will be something different for us. It will be a more professional direction for us where we can create a first-rate gallery space."

Drawing Rooms Curator, Anne Trauben, planned one last big and exciting show before moving, and wanted it to be inclusive where any artist- local, national or international, could participate. Director Jim Pustorino suggested Edgar Allan Poe's "The Mask of Red Death." as the theme because the story follows a group of wealthy people who have an exclusive party in the abbey where each room is a different color.

In Somewhere Over the Interconnected Rainbow and Prospero's Grand Street Masque, each room in the convent featured painting and drawing by nearly 200 artists from as far away as Scotland and France and the artwork in each room was grouped by color. Close to 300 works were pinned to a wire running the length of the room. Artwork was for sale for $200 each, and collectors could pick up the work they purchased after the show or have it mailed to them. In addition to the artwork, Saturday night's event featured live music, sushi from Komegashi restaurant, refreshments, and party masks.

Saturday's exhibition took place from 7 p.m. to 10 p.m. and Sunday's ran from 12 p.m. to 4 p.m. with a closing brunch. While the event was free, donations were encouraged and appreciated for anyone visiting the exhibit. All the proceeds from the show would go to build Drawing Rooms' new space in the Topps Building. First exhibit in the new space was planned for Fall.

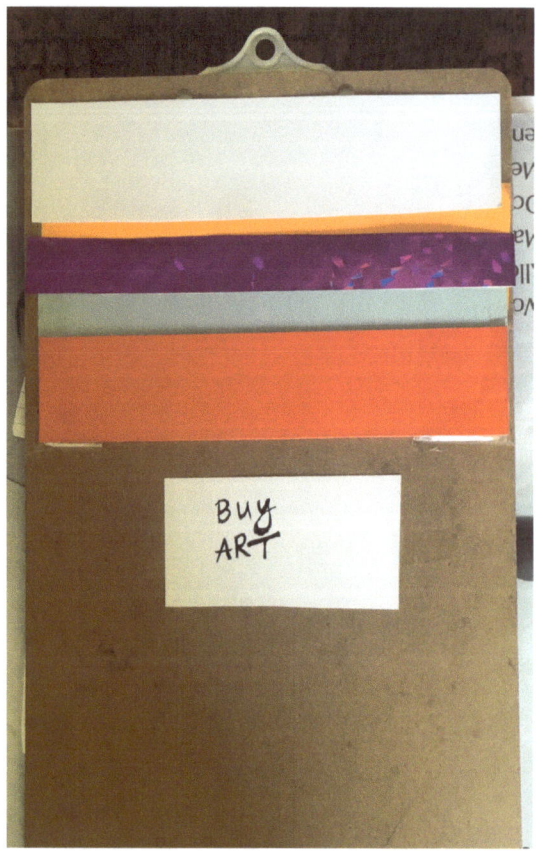

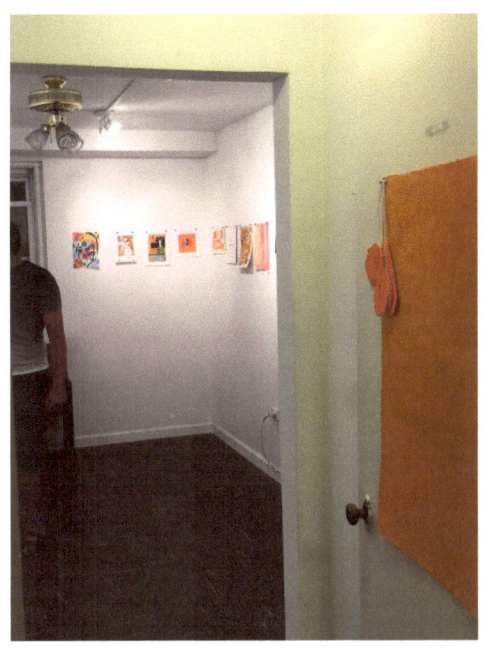
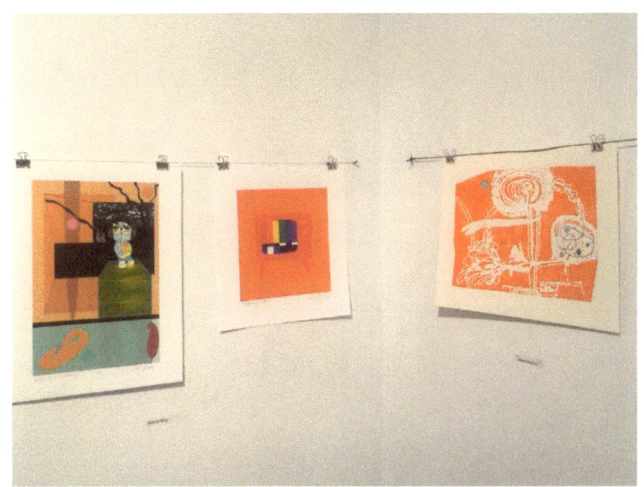

ORANGE

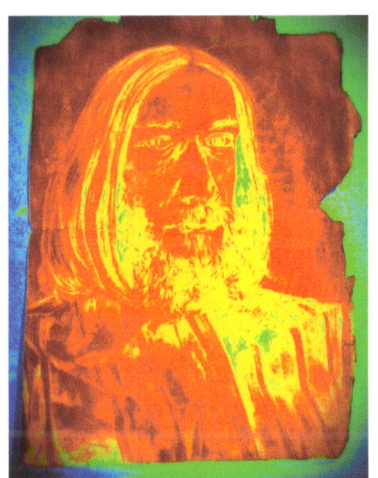
Greg Stone

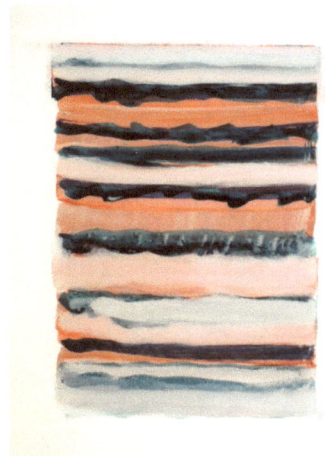
Emily Berger

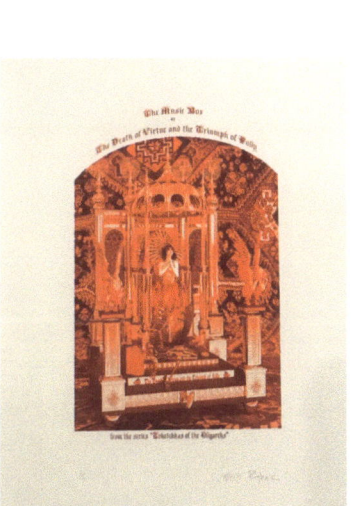
Bill Rybak

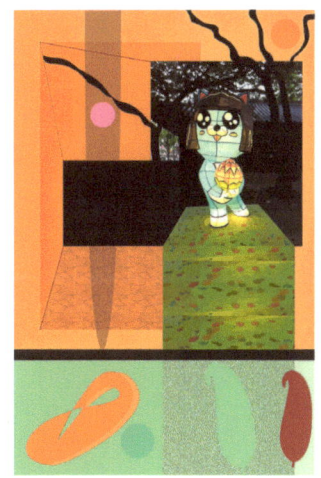
Beatrice Mady

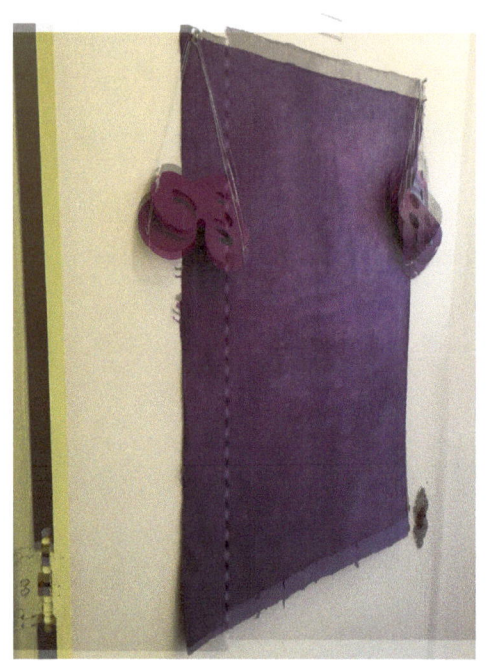
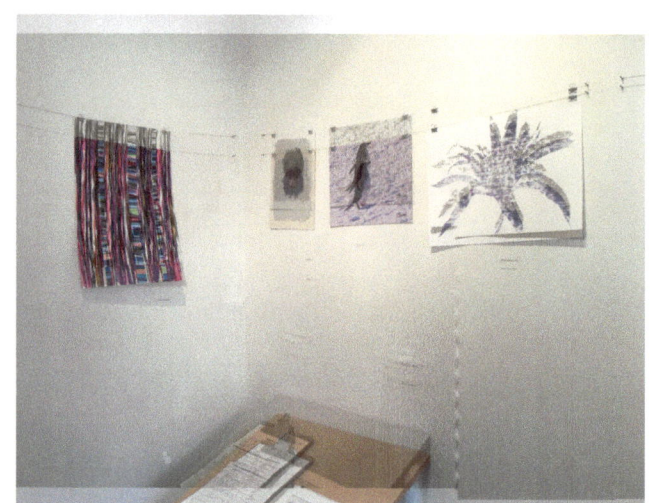

PURPLE

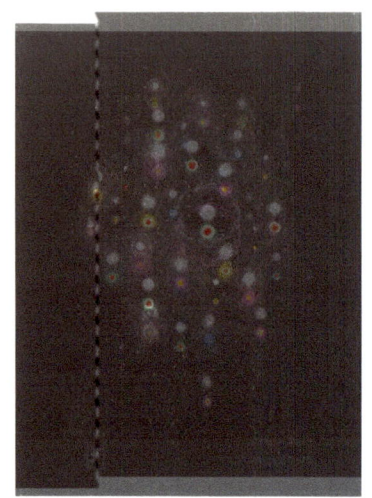

Bill Stamos

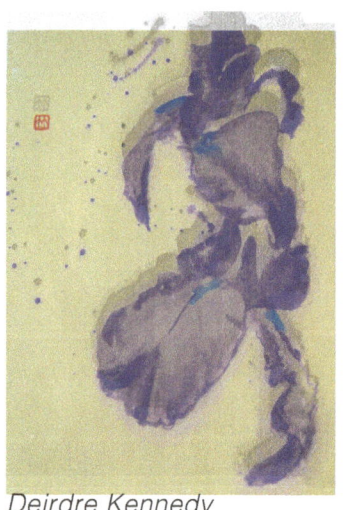

Deirdre Kennedy

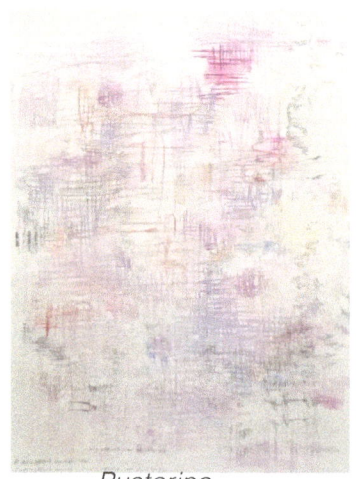

James Pustorino

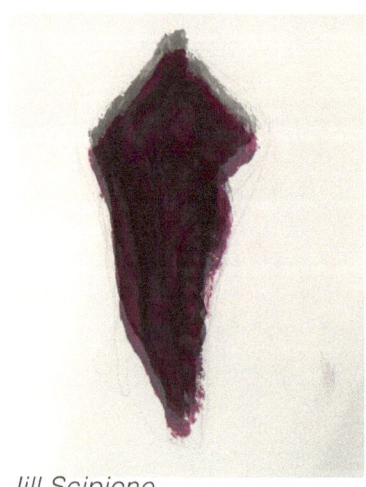

Jill Scipione

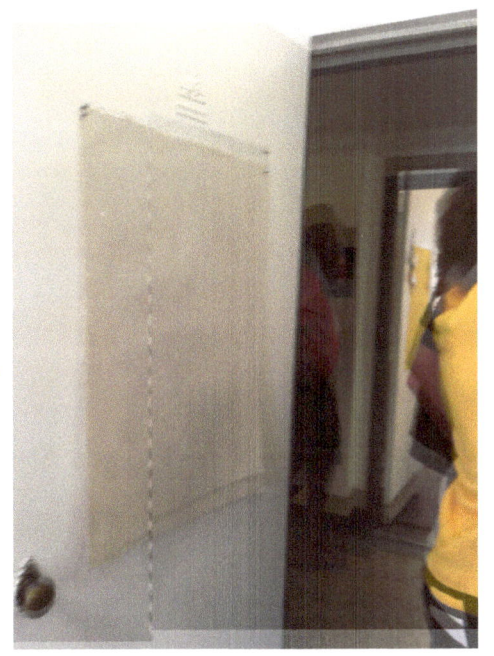
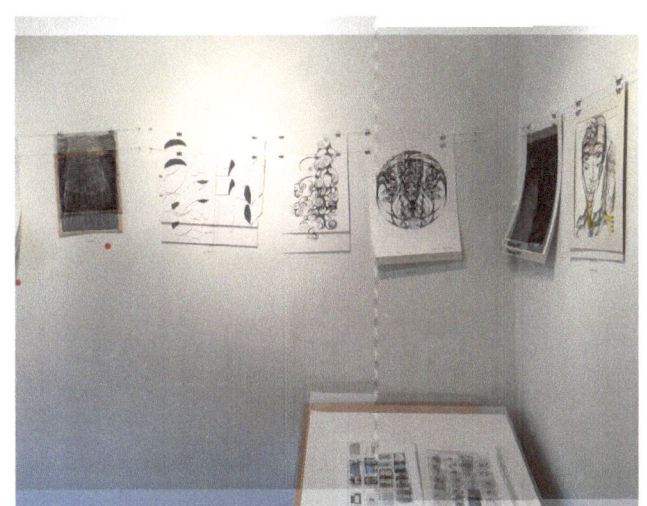

WHITE

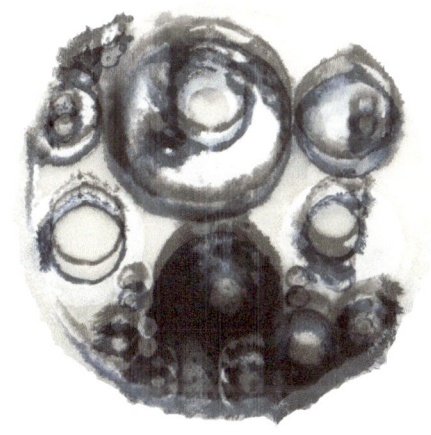

Beth Dary

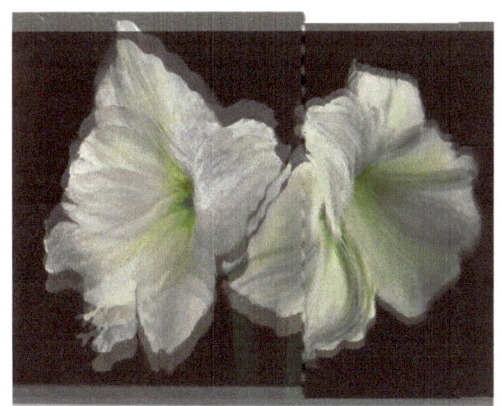

Joan Marie Palmer

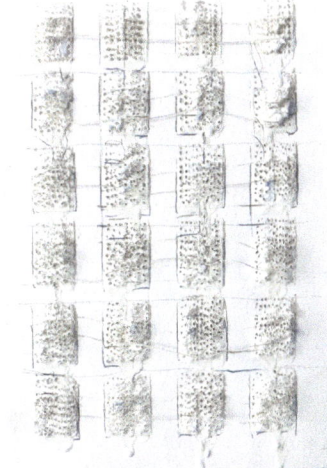

Megan Klim

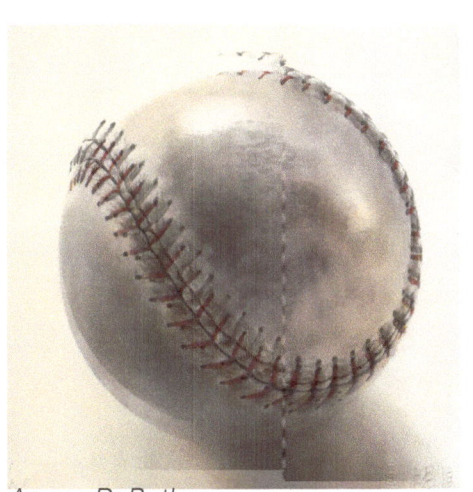

Agnes DeBethune

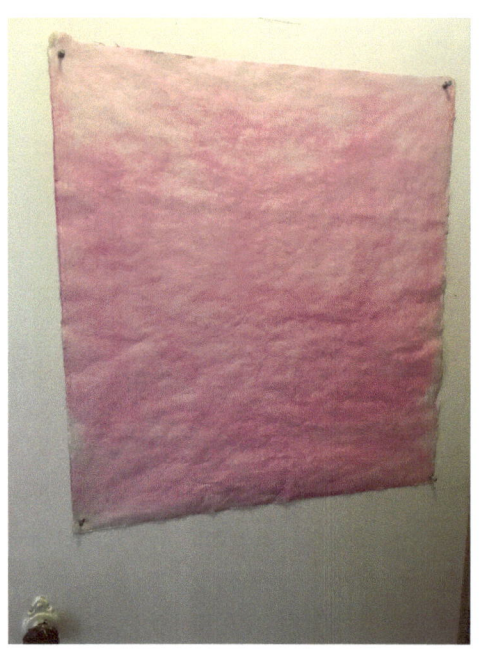
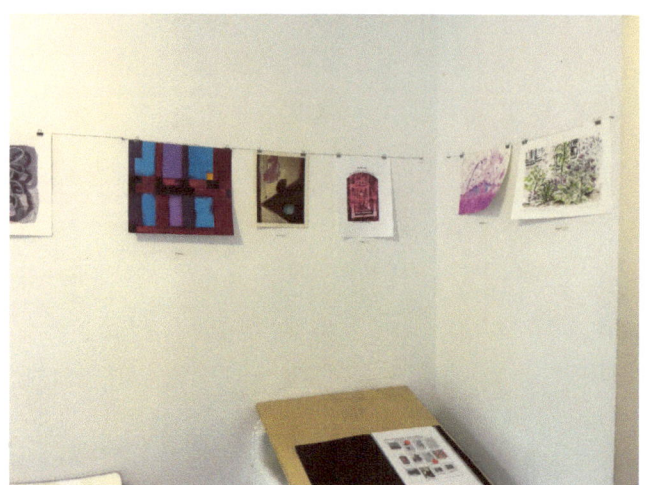

VIOLET

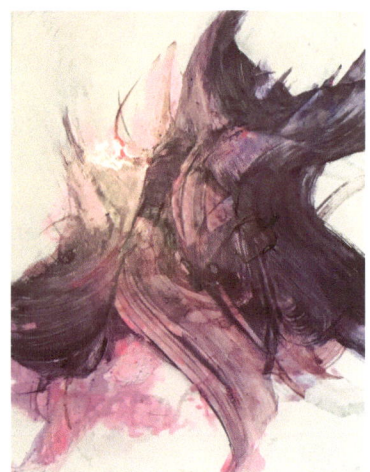

Bithika Adhikary

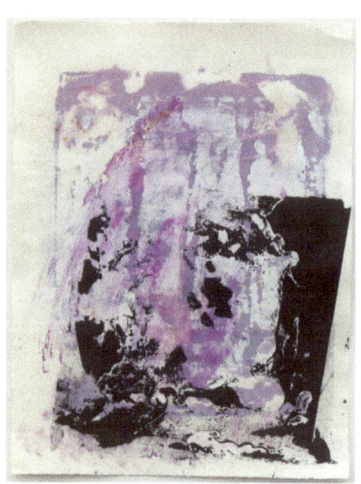

Rich White

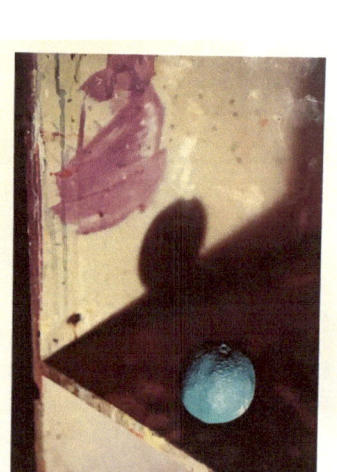

Elaine Hansen

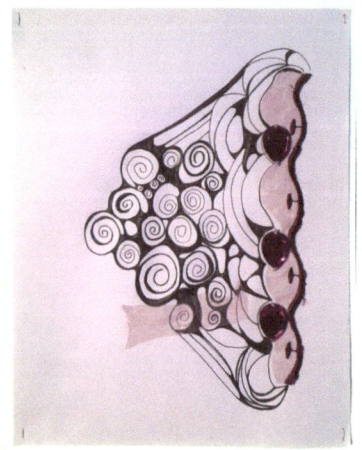

Anne Trauben

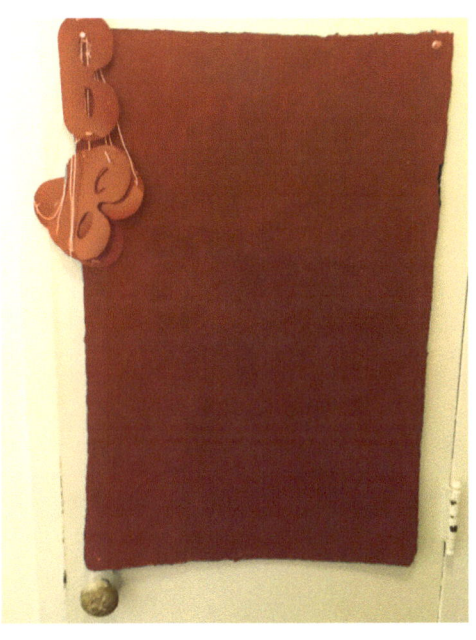
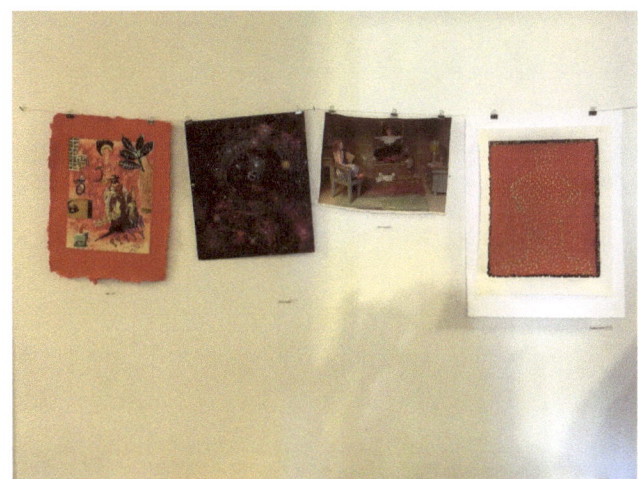

RED

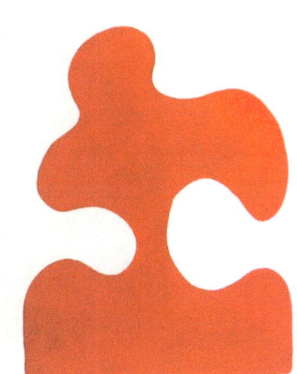

Dana Kane

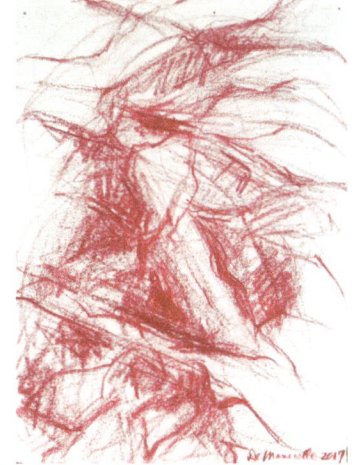

Stephanie DeManuelle

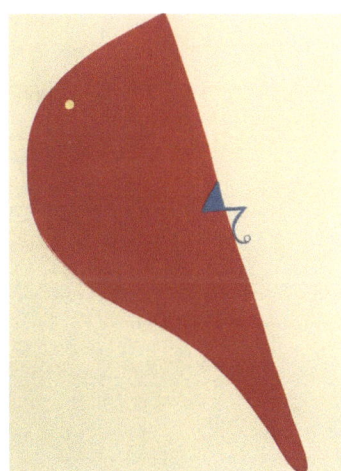

Pauline Galiana

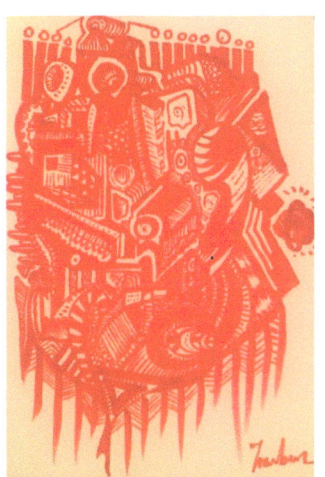

Jackson Trauben

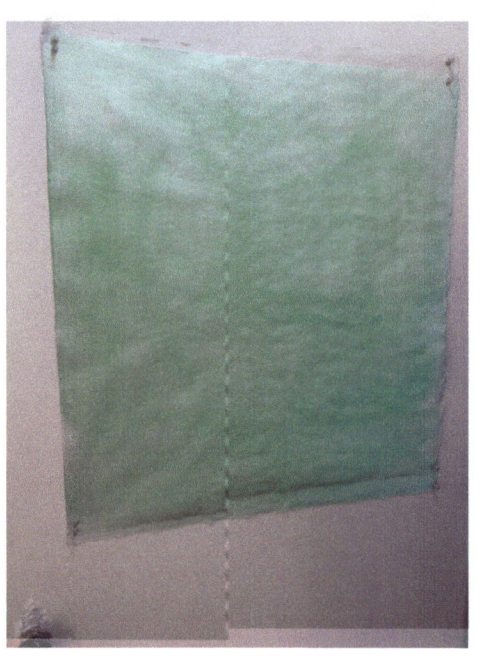
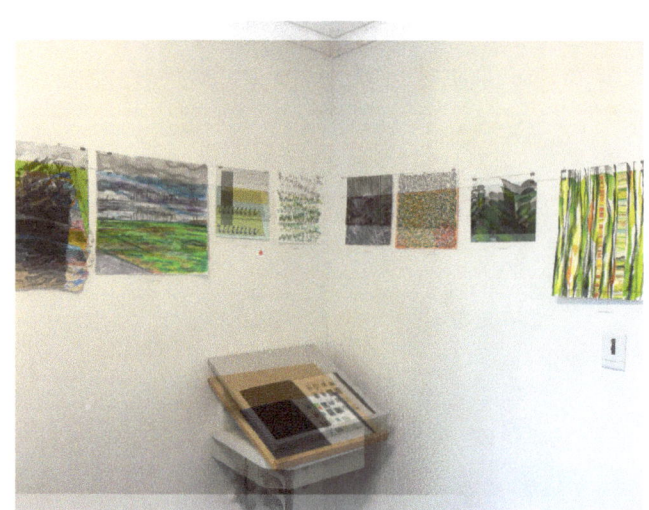

GREEN

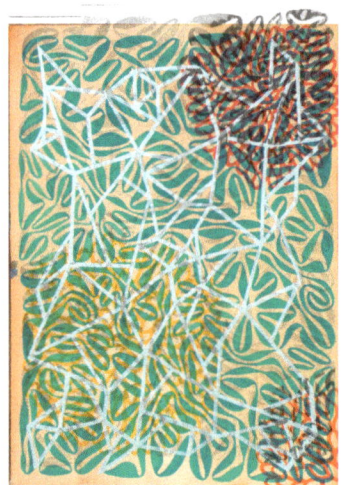

Patricia Fabricant

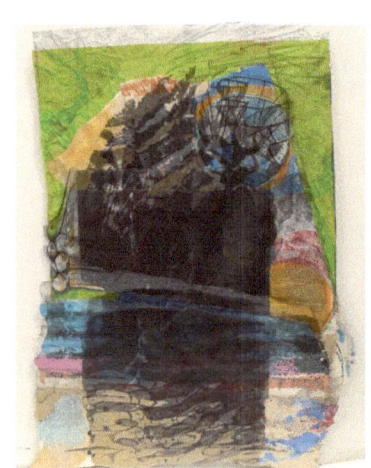

Ani Roskam

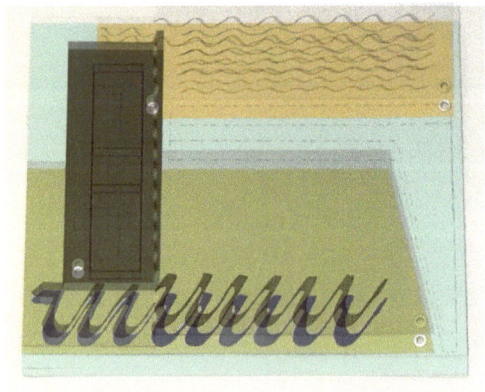

Jim Osman

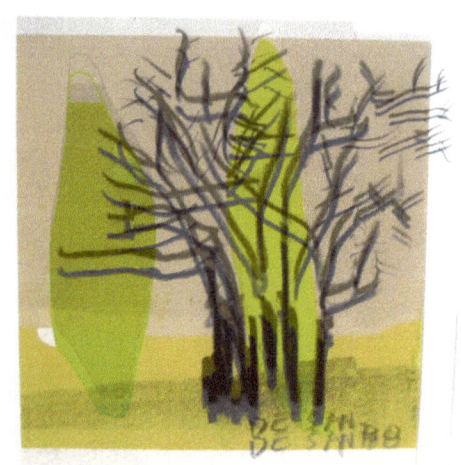

Sandra DeSando

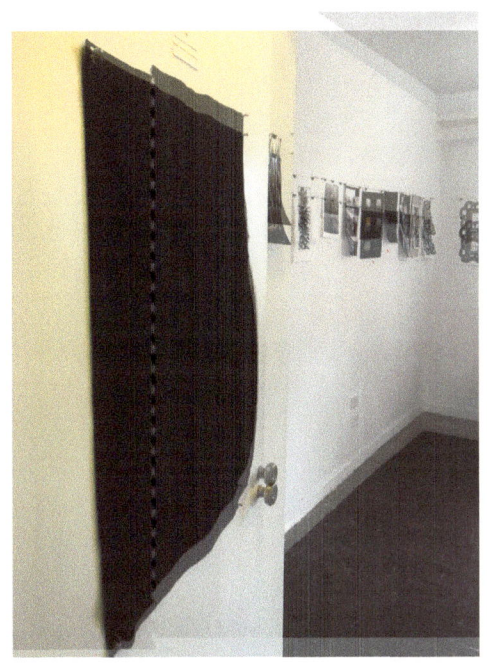
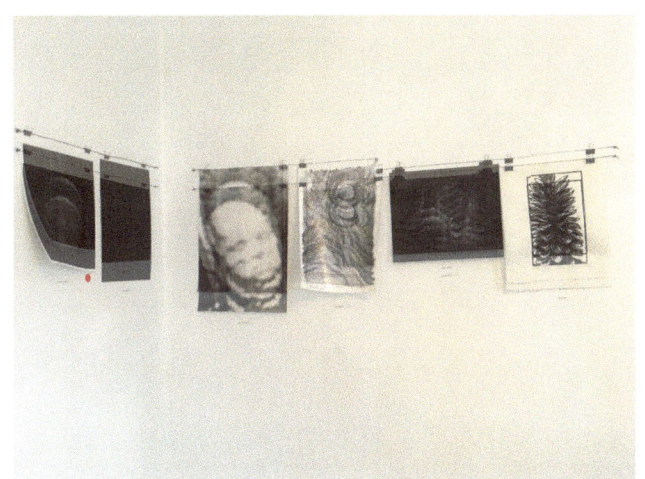

BLACK

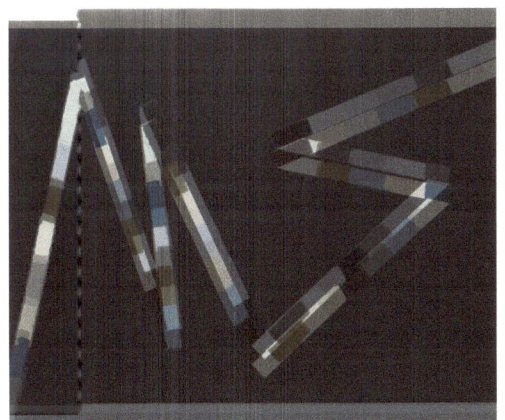

Kathy Cantwell

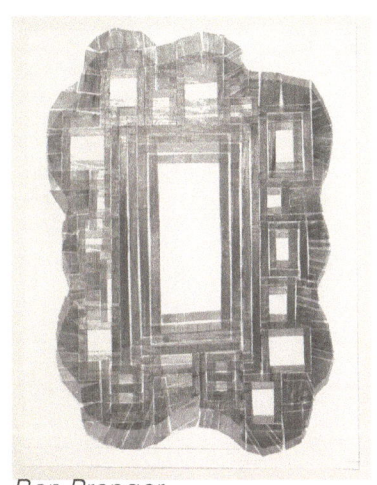

Ben Pranger

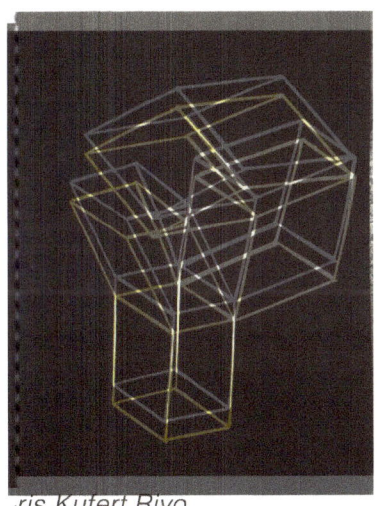

Iris Kufert Rivo

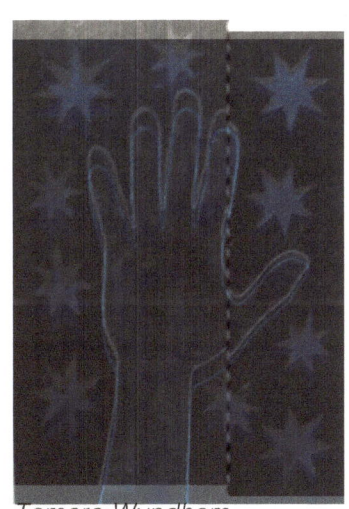

Tamara Wyndham

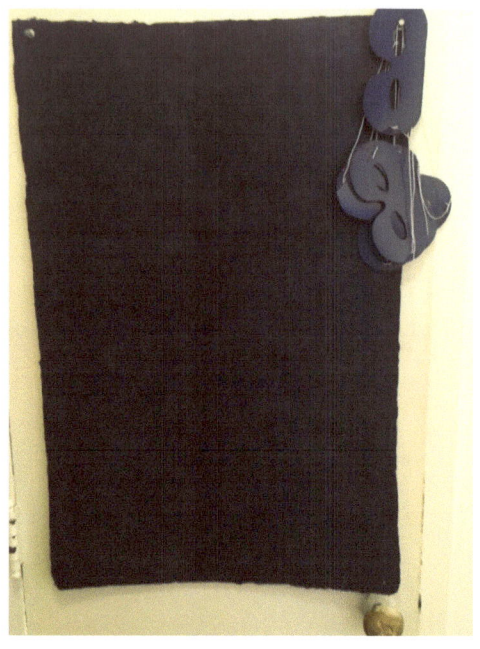
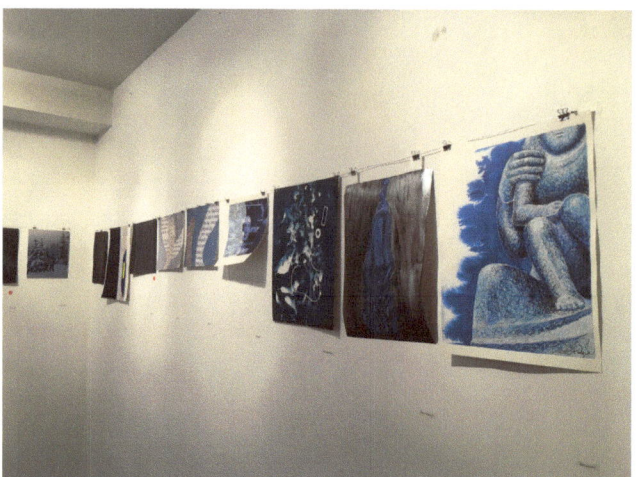

BLUE

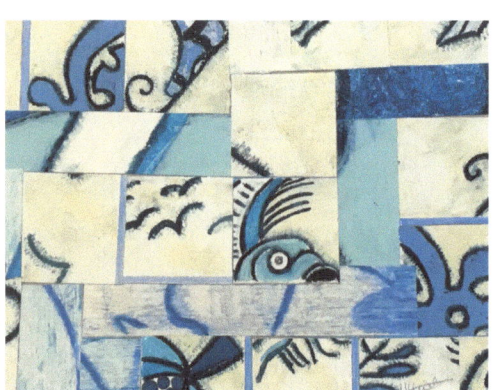

Loura van der Meule

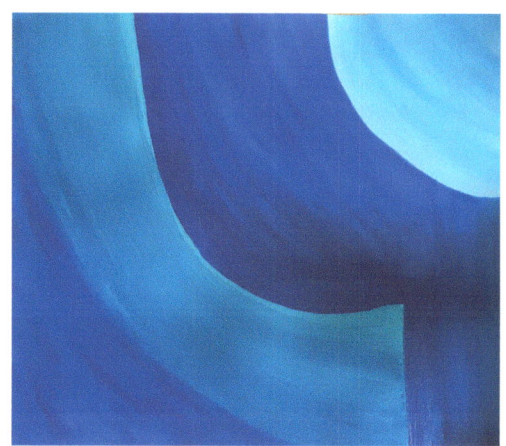

Alberte Bernier

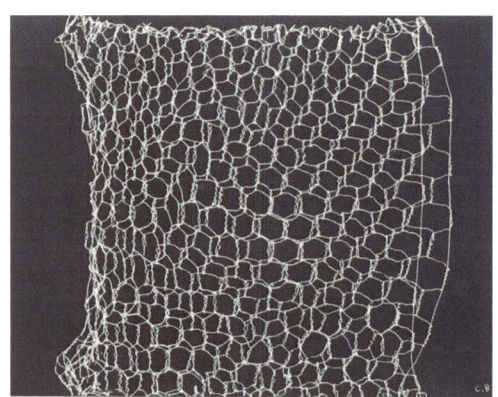

Caroline Burton

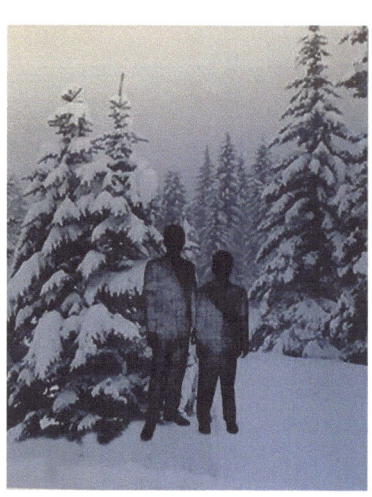

Eugenio Espinoza

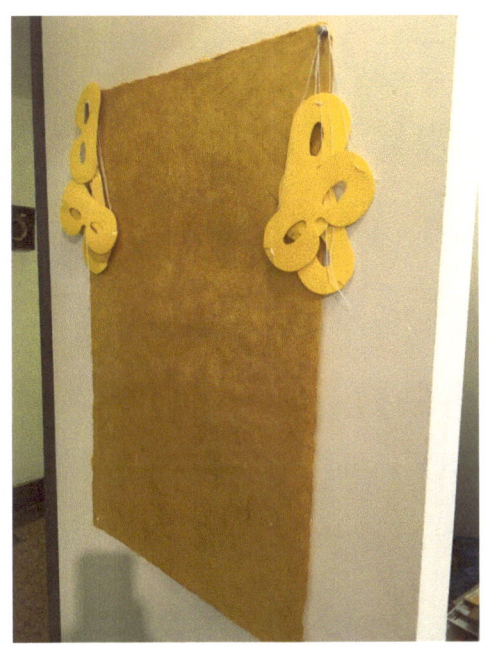
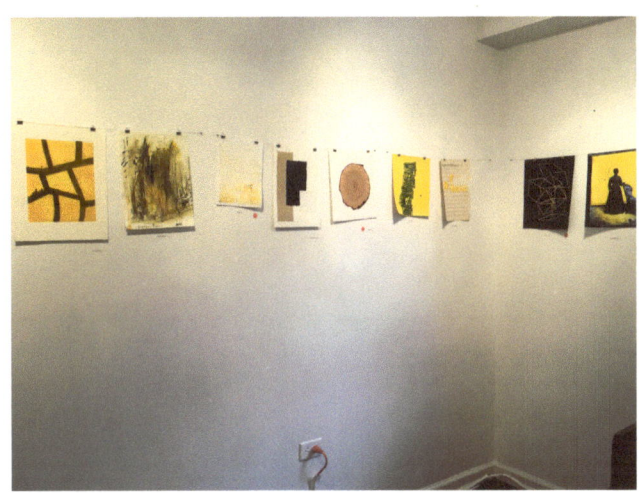

YELLOW

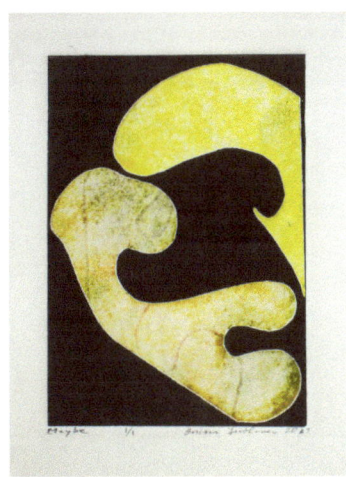

Barbara Lubliner

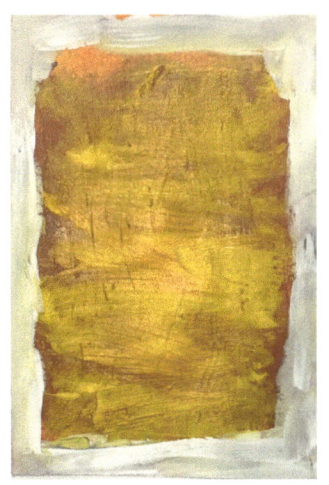

Marianne DeAngelis

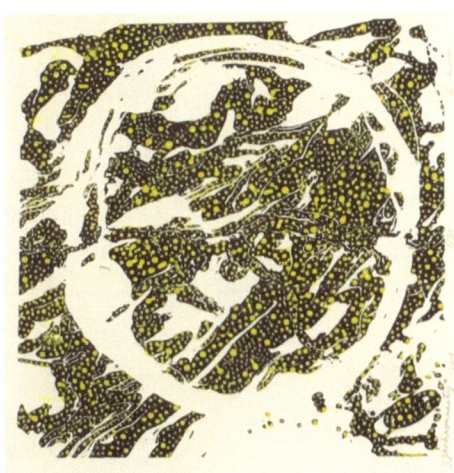

Anthony Boone

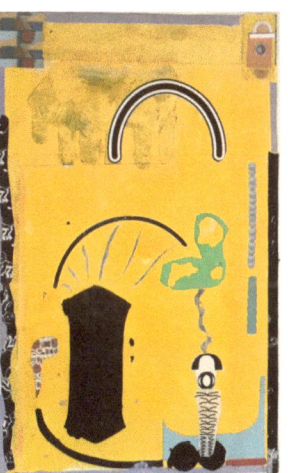

Bill Leech

Now Ya See it Now Ya Don't / Open and Shut / Sneak Peak / Not Ready for Prime Time / This is Not the Grand Opening: Drawing Rooms Presents The Artists of the Topps Building

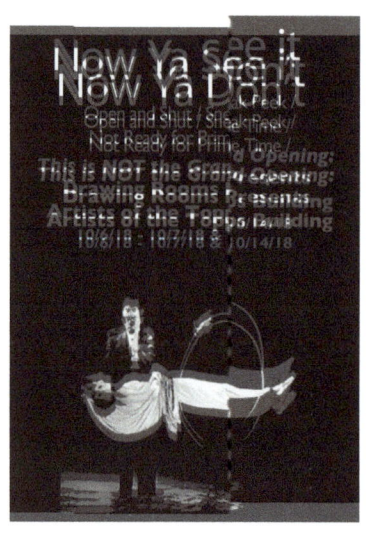
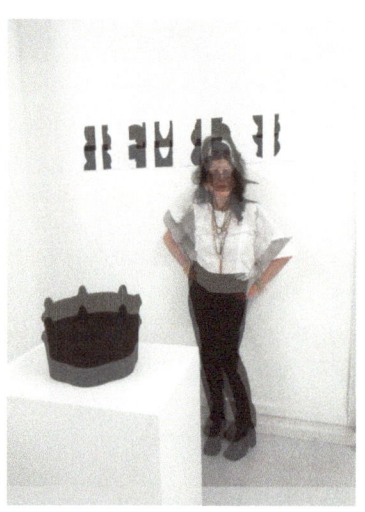
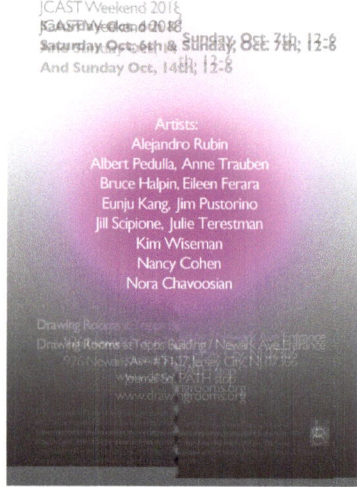

Now Ya See it Now Ya Don't / Open and Shut / Sneak Peak / Not Ready for Prime Time / This is Not the Grand Opening: Drawing Rooms Presents The Artists of the Topps Building
10/6/18-10/7/18 & 10/14/18

Drawing Rooms invited friends, artists and art-goers for a two-weekend peek at our almost finished new gallery in the Topps building on the Mana campus. After a successful spring fundraiser show, we spent the summer planning and building the galleries in our new space and made good progress. Although we were not ready to begin our regular exhibit season, we made good on our plan to open the space up and put some artwork on our new walls for the Jersey City Studio Tour.

In addition to presenting works from the artists who run Drawing Rooms, we were excited to feature works by many of the artists at the Topps Building, some of whom we have exhibited over the past years, as well as some who are new to us. In the works in this show, chosen by Curator Anne Trauben, color, texture and form communicate with power and elegance.

In the large front gallery, **James Pustorino** presented a set of oil on vinyl paintings from the late 1990s that relied on the groovy graphic design he grew up with in the late 1960's and 70's. Flowing reds, pinks oranges and yellows dominated these wall-size, flame-like images.

Kimberley Wiseman's self-portrait looked on from the next gallery room with brilliantly colored curving forms that seemed to sculpt themselves into face hair and clothing.

This second gallery featured one of **Nancy Cohen's** large-scale paper compositions. Nancy has developed a unique body of work by creating complex, two-dimensional "drawings" or "paintings" using paper and hand-made

30 Exhibitions

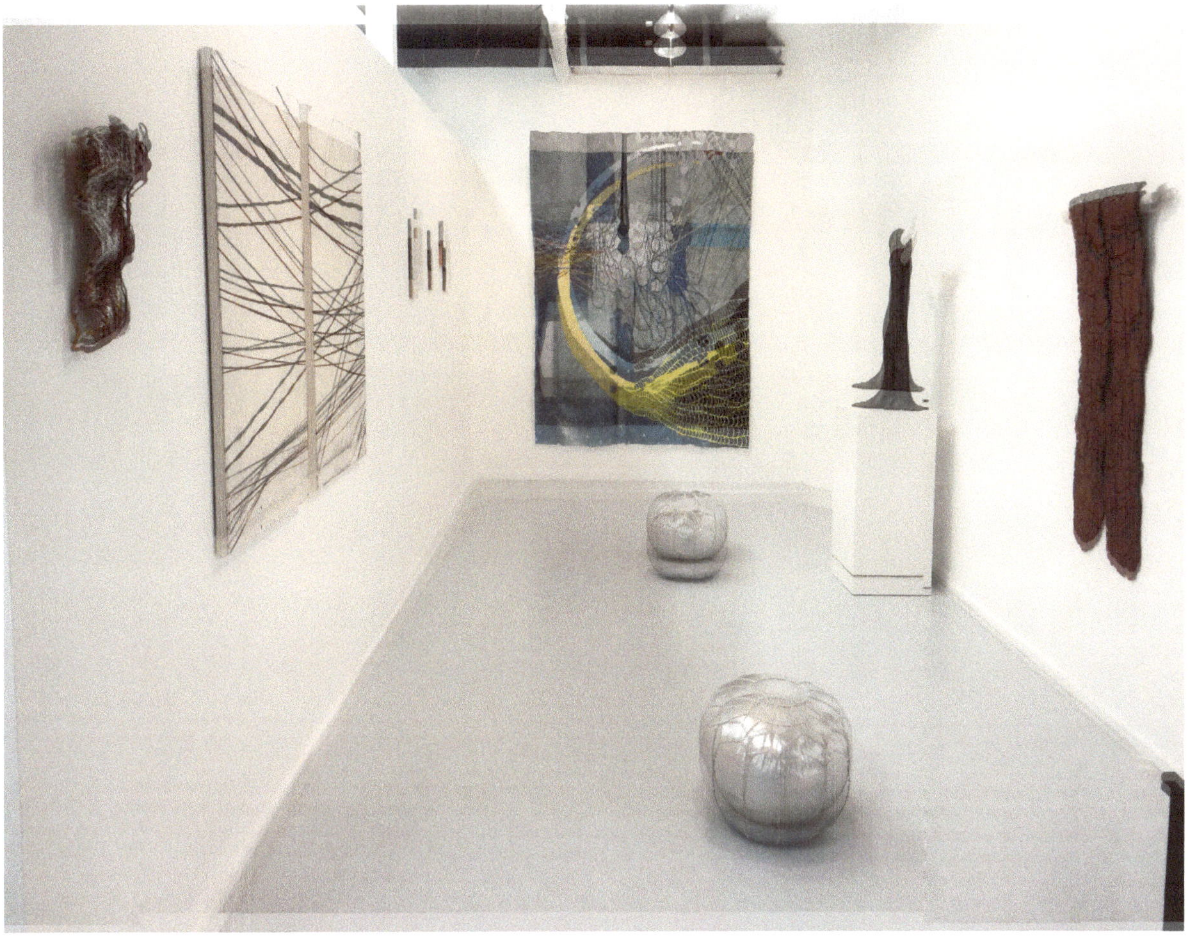

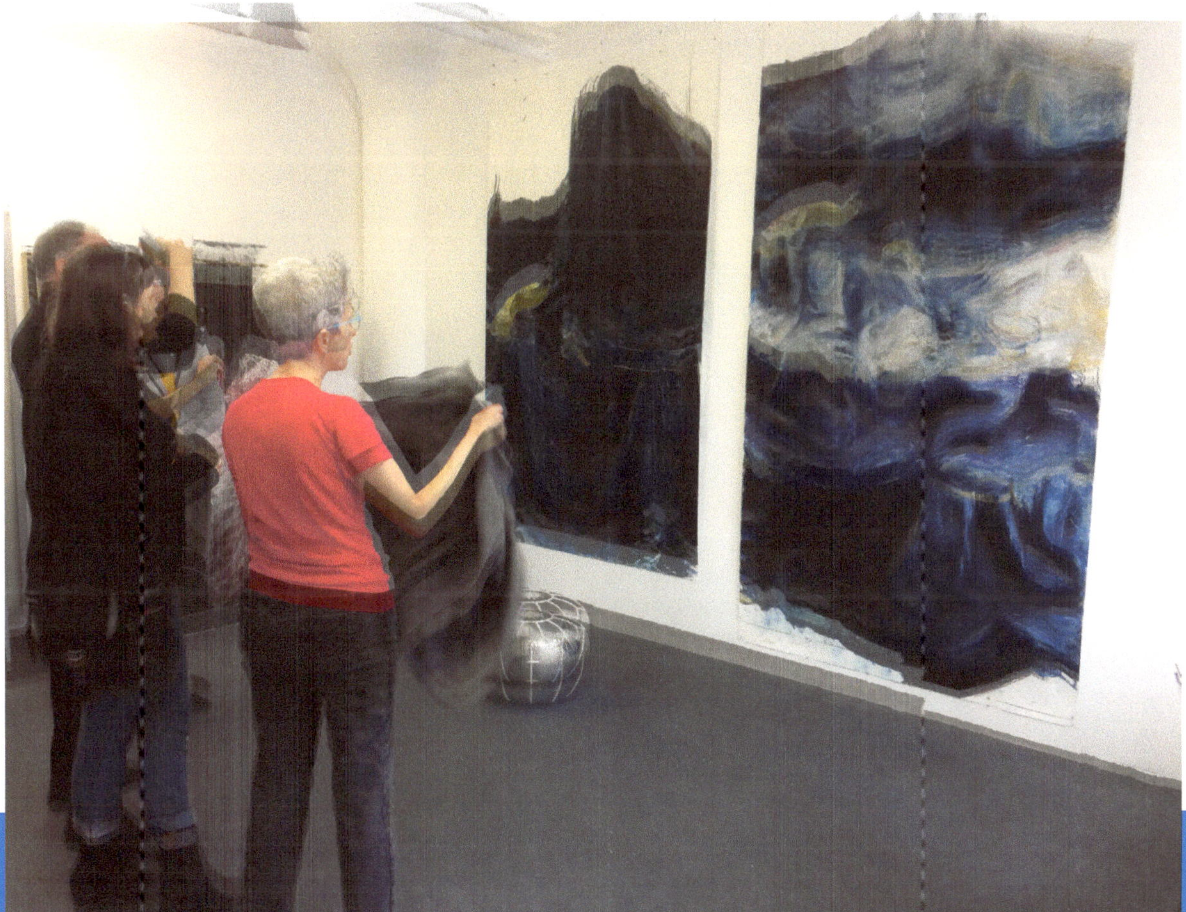

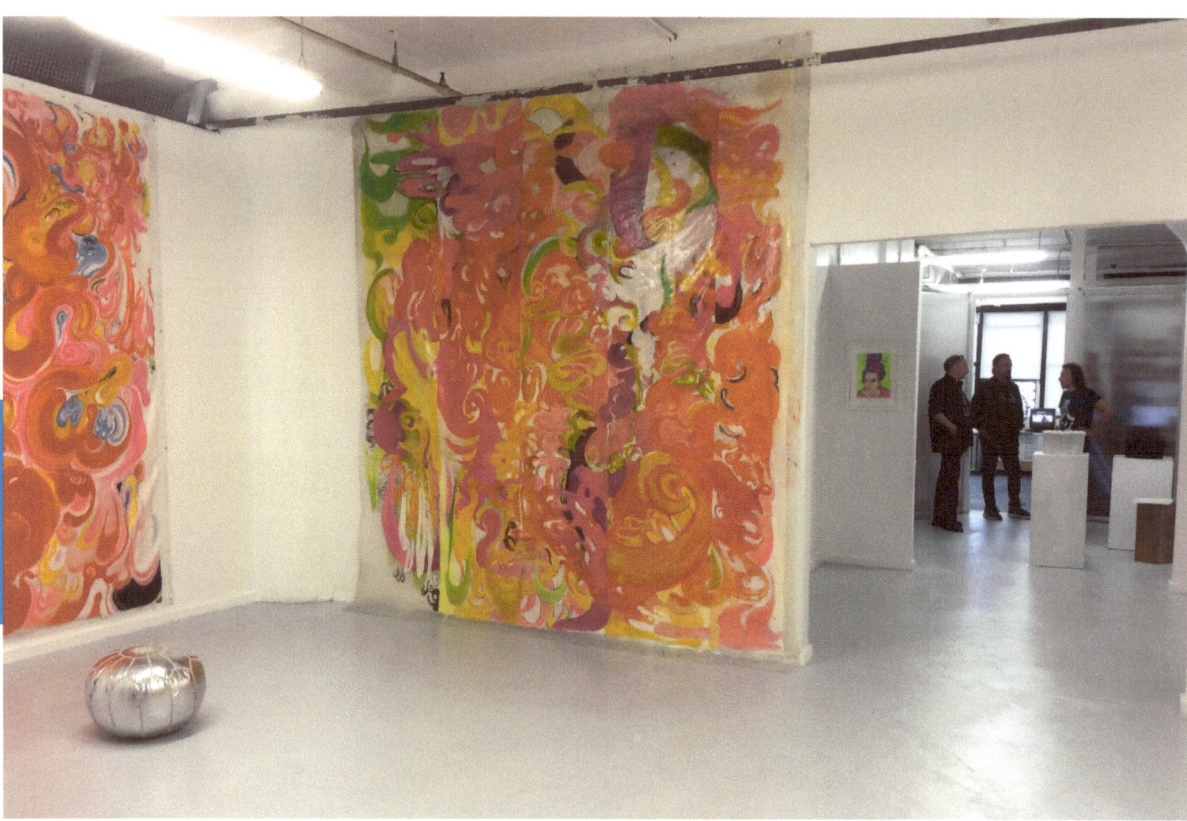

extruded paper pulp. The rich and varied tones and textures of the papers and the ability to 'draw' and layer lines and shapes of brilliant color with precise clarity allow her nature-based abstractions to become fully realized.

Opposite this work, **Eunju Kang** also created what appeared to be an abstract painting out of colored paper. Eunju assembled thousands of tiny strips of multi-colored paper into vertical, horizontal and diagonal areas that might resemble the layout of fields or city lots. She then dramatically broke the pattern with what at first appeared to be running drips of white paint- but this is then revealed to be carefully cut-out blank spaces.

Albert Pedulla's elegant photo-image of electric lines in quiet off-white's and sepa-blacks was presented on two canvas panels like a minimalist diptych painting. Next to these, **Bruce Halpin's** three small works of paint on rectangles of wood are likewise elegant, minimal and softly toned. The rough edges of his wood blocks work against the measured balance of his hard-edge geometry. In **Nora Chavoosian's** sculptures, artificial materials, such as pvc pipes and resins, become horns and cracked earth in these simple, yet animated objects, emphasising texture and natural form.

In **Anne Trauben's** twenty-eight small oil pastel drawings, she shapes black and white into positive/negative arrangements acting like musical notes, or letters in an abstract sentence that circuites the room. Her work surrounds two of **Julie Terestman's** large clay vessels, one black one white. The tactile, rough texture of the outside of these complex rings contrast sharply with the shiny colorful interior.

In the last room, **Jill Scipione's** large oil pastel drawings describe masses of deep dark blue-black, forms that could be water or cloth or land, shot through with occasional bursts of golden light and cast like a shadow against the stark white paper. **Alejandro Rubin's** video, in the same room, is as much about the color red as Scipione's is about blue. In it, we see his students responding to his story about that color as they draw and write with an earthy red pigment and then are recorded as they wash it away. Floating blue forms create a peaceful balance in **Eileen Ferara's** prints and drawings that emulate the visual rhythm of nature.

The exhibit was part of the Jersey City Artists Studio Tour and continued through the next weekend, joining with Mana Contemporary's open house event.

The Art Project

Victory Hall Inc. Director James Pustorino works throughout the year with Shuster Development, to establish The Art Project in downtown Jersey City. Artists from Jersey City and beyond are currently exhibiting in the forty lobby areas in the three public and residential buildings that the company has built or renovated since 2014.

The goal of the project is to support and promote the artists in Jersey City's Powerhouse Arts District by selling their creations. All proceeds directly benefit the artist, and a meaningful portion goes back into the community for arts programming.

The buildings are designed to provide viewing areas, lighting and wall space so that each floor acts as an small art gallery dedicated to displaying the work of a specific artist. Tours of all lobby-gallery floors in the buildings are given during JC Friday evenings four times a year, and during the Jersey City Studio Tour weekend in October.

All artworks are available for purchase at **www.drawingrooms.org**.

If you are interested in taking a tour in the building, buying an artwork or if you are an artist interested in submitting your work please contact: **victoryhall1@msn.com**.

Noyes Museum, Drawing Rooms Art Project: JC in AC

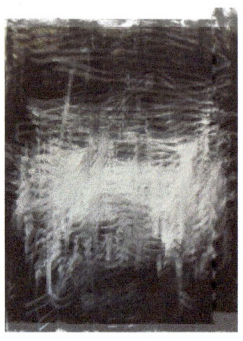 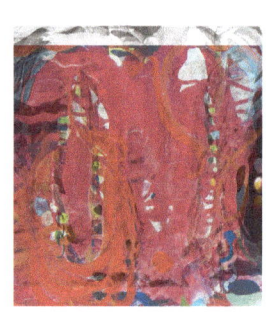 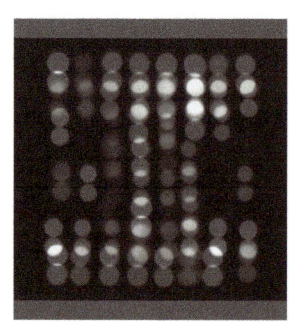 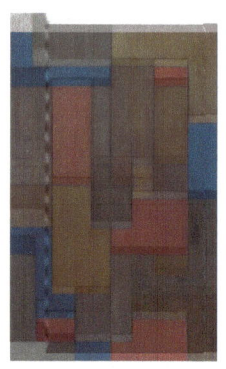

Drawing Rooms Art Project: JC in AC
April 5-June 6
Noyes Art Garage

Artists who participated in Drawing Rooms' Art Project, Victory Hall's Art in Public Places program that fills almost forty lobbies in four buildings with vibrant and innovative works, were featured in a visually stunning exhibition at Noyes this past Spring. Sparse black and white forms, energized slashes and bursts of marks, patterns and glowing colors made up the visual language and strong graphic impact of the works by this group of New Jersey artists.

"Noyes Garage is the perfect place to expose these artists to the AC public and get people of all ages to see what artists working in their state are making, and for the artists to meet the public, and get a response to their work. The accessible, relaxed atmosphere at Noyes makes art part of everyone's daily life, which is how it should be," says the curator and also artist, Anne Trauben.

Alejandro Rubin's "Just Keep Swimming" photo series shares his love of the water with the viewer. Saturated in color and mesmerising pattern, the images become abstract and emotive. Born and raised in Caracas, Venezuela (where he took these pictures), Alejandro moved to the United States after finishing high school with academic and athletic scholarships to pursue a degree in Graphic Design and Photography, and be part of the Swimming team at Saint Peter's University. He is currently working on his MFA at NJCU in Jersey City and is an Intern at Drawing Rooms.

Alyce Gottesman, a NJ native, says the rhythms of the seasons and the energy of nature influences her work, as well as and the special light that exists in N. California where she spent the latter part of her childhood. Alyce cites her lifelong appreciation of music as another influences her painting. Alyce made these paintings when she returned from a recent trip to India.

Anne Trauben is a sculptor who seeks to blur the line between two and three dimensions in her work. She is always considering formal design elements such as the beauty of shapes and how one shapes connects to another. Her 24 minimal collages are installed in a grid that take up a full wall. Anne says she "found such pleasure in cutting the forms with a scissor, as though I'm drawing in space or refining the curve of a clay form", and asks us to consider "how many ways can an idea be expressed differently"?

Bruce Halpin says his "relationship with painting is complex and contradictory". His flat, yet creamy, mat paintings on wood constructions become intriguing graphic/architectural objects. Connecting to nature has long been a source of inspiration and is reflected in the work of **Eileen Ferara**. Using a mix of materials and techniques, Eileen's works involve printmaking, collage,

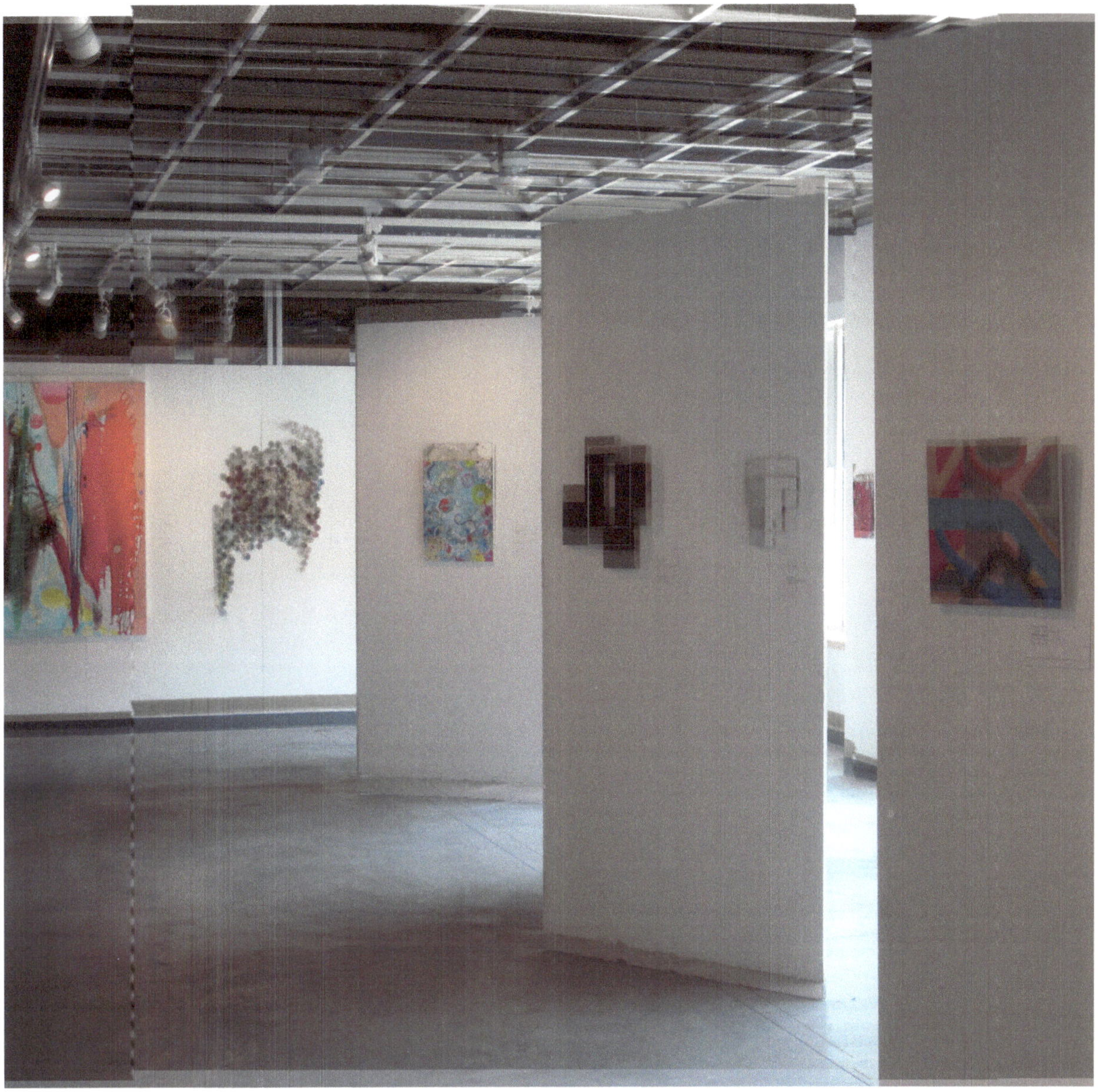

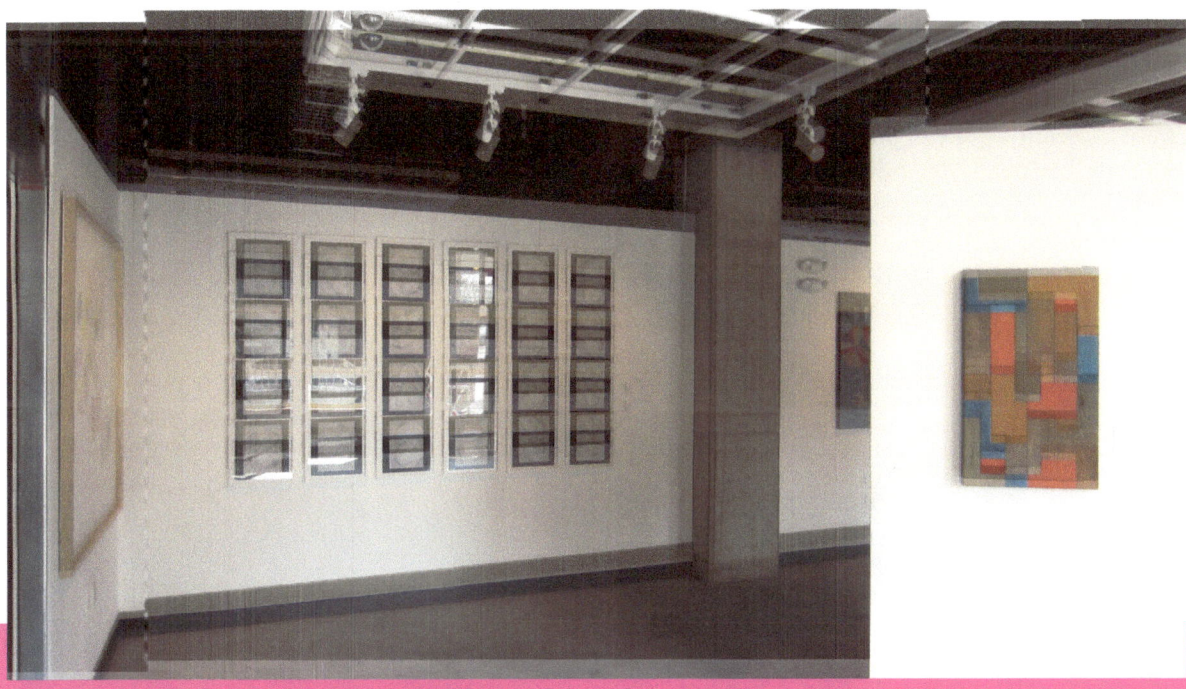

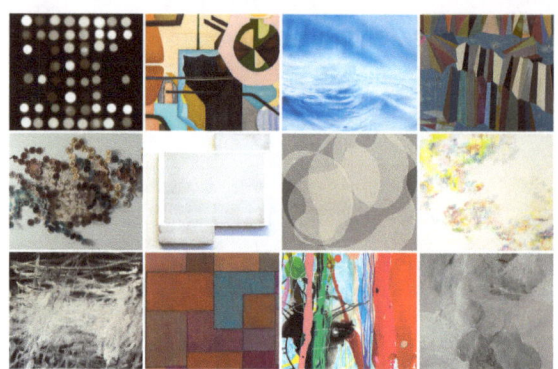

artist's books and painting. Her recent work has been an exploration of her relationship to the environment of the Estuary, specifically, the local urban waterways around the Hudson River, and surrounding marsh areas which empty out into the Atlantic Ocean.

Greg Letson's work explores ways of "expressing emotions, concepts, ideas and stories through a reductive vocabulary of visual shapes, marks and structures". Greg's images are "never preconceived and are always a product of an unfolding sequence of impulses and decisions in the course of making each final image". Greg's paintings "exist solely as visual compositions which are meant to resonate uniquely within the perceptual faculties of each viewer".

Jill Scipione presents dynamic, large-scale paintings inspired by passages from the Biblical Psalms and books of the Old Testament Prophets. Jill's paintings are about light traced into dark; her drawing line becoming a painted trail of movement, creating and diffusing figures, forms and atmospheres. Her themes of Tent, Snare, Scaffolding, Messenger and Survival Suit, speak of threat and protection, fear and safety, destruction and deliverance.

James Pustorino's Every Second Counted series uses short color strokes and a "scribbled" line to build up form. According to Jim, "this composition can approximate music in that it is built of marks of color drawn with varying strengths, speeds and emphasis much like musical notes and tones or the way different instruments work together in a musical composition. As in music, structure and form are built through repetition, variation and contrast, areas of intensity and areas of rest; and the creation of an engrossing or compelling visual experience, as opposed to aural experience, is the goal of the piece."

Karen Nielsen-Fried's Intuitive Geometries series explores the beauty of geometric form as well as "random expansion of those forms to create entities that have emotional narrative". "The Self is made up of all of the scraps of moments of being. We try to put forward a seamless facade as we tell ourselves and others our story."

"The intentional quality of the sublime emerges at the heart of this work" by **Mona Brody**. Her "personal experience, writings, and biography shape the nature of many of the works, always encouraging viewers to think about their own associations with themes of memory, personal histories, and time."

Photographer **Roger Sayre**, creates unique images with a strong sense of design through inventive photo-techniques. His photo "Buenos Aires (Bobby Fischer vs Tigran Vartanovich Petrosian, 1971 - Fischer in 34 moves)" is a document of every move from the thrilling championship chess game. Moving real chess pieces in actual-time chess moves on photosensitive paper, Sayre's layered dark and light chessboard becomes a shadowy memory of the moments of the game.

For more than a decade, **Stephen Cimini's** oil paint with cold wax medium painting has been inspired by architecture. Stephen has started referring to his compositions as "random symmetry" where he "creates a balance on the canvas with no discernible pattern allowing a symmetrical, meditative composition to emerge". Stephen uses the golden mean as a reference in his work.

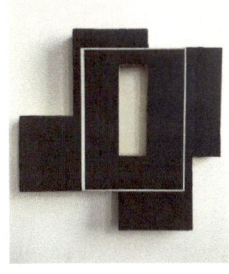
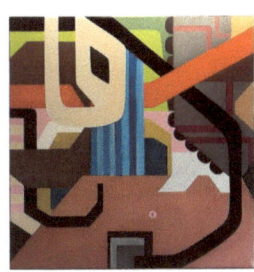
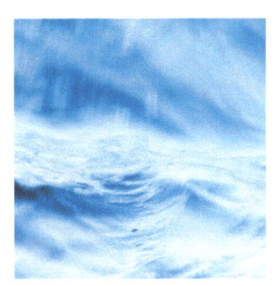
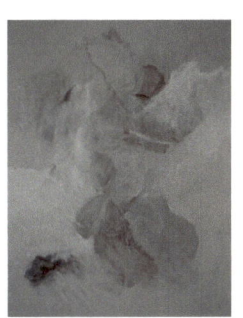
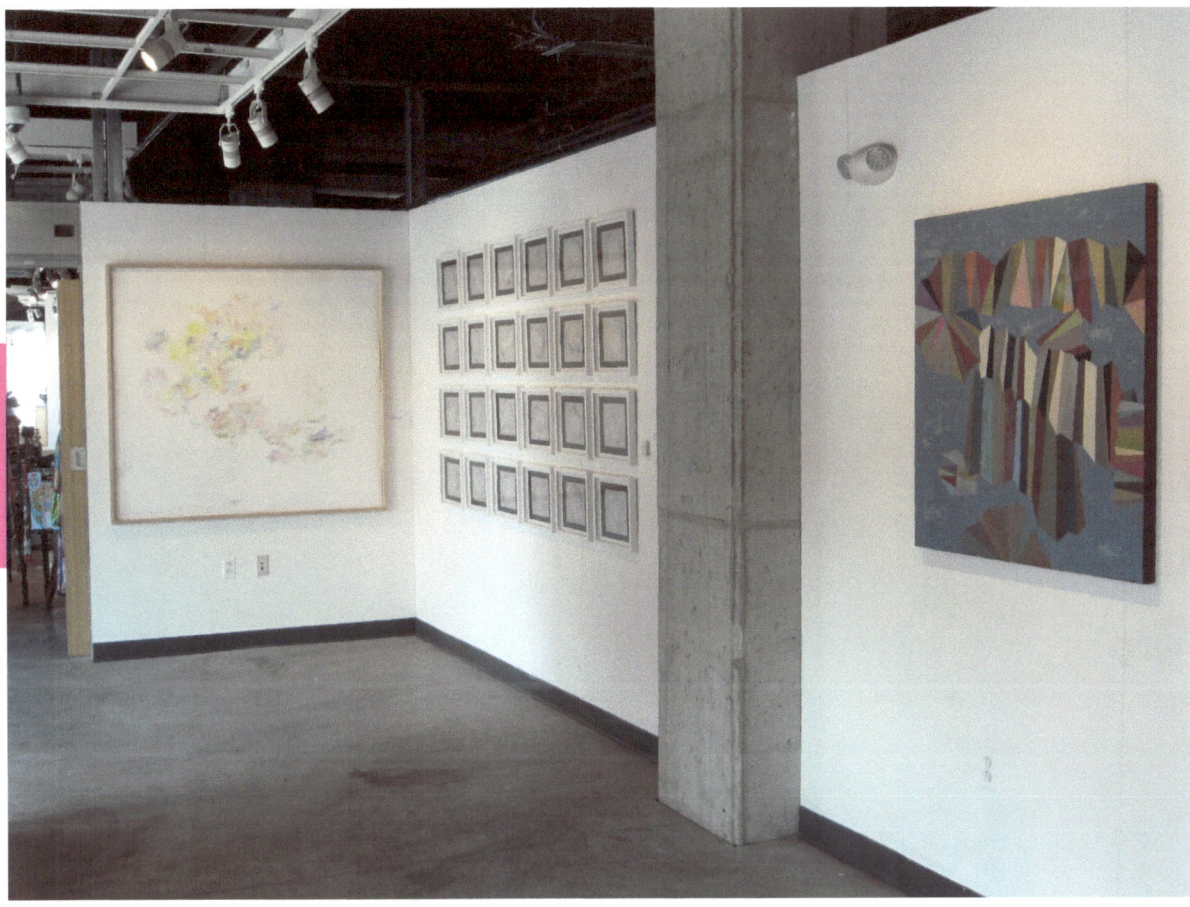
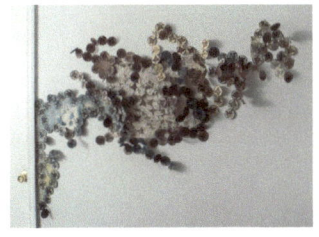
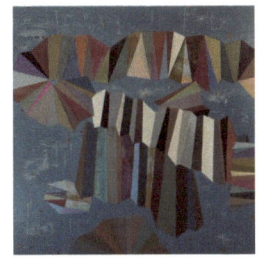
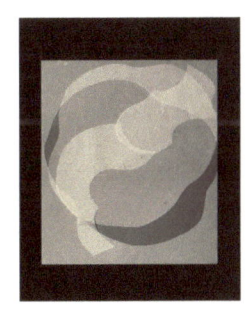
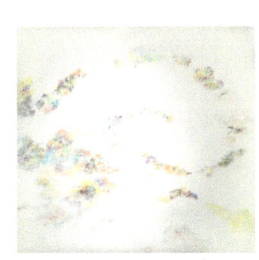

Gallery 109 Columbus - 109 Columbus Dr. Jersey City

The spacious two-tiered gallery at 109 Columbus Drive, JC is open with year round exhibitions and has been the site for our annual Holiday Fundraiser. **2018 exhibitions featured artists:** Greg Brickey, Harriet Finck, Bruce Halpin, David French and Sandra DeSando.

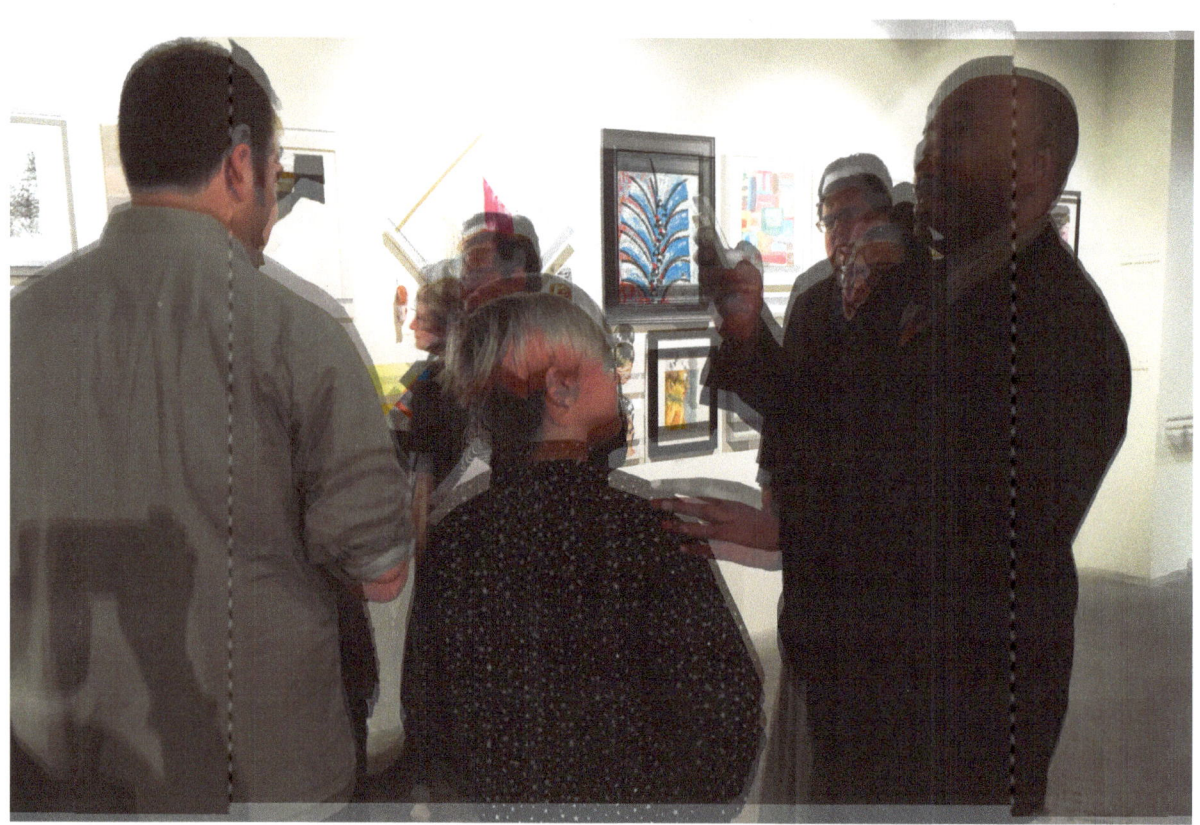

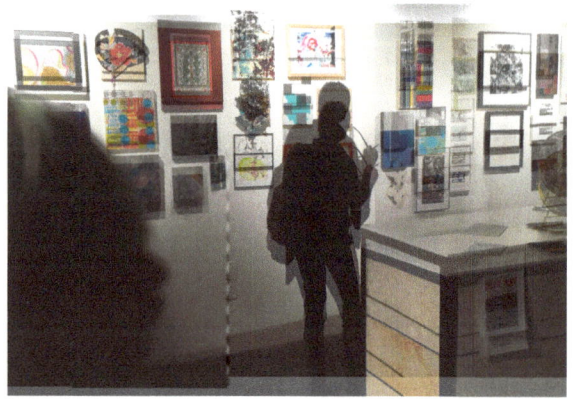
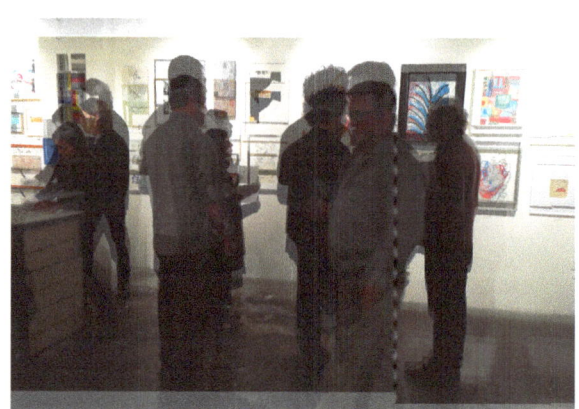

The Oakman - 160 First St. Jersey City

Artists: Jodie Fink, Geoffrey Sokol, Deanna Lee, Susan Cornick, Natalie Giugni, Rich White, Linda Gottesfeld, Bithika Adhikary, Nancy Karpf, Yael Dresdner, Peter Delman, Alpana Mittal, Lisa Collodoro, Joe Lugara, and James Pustorino.

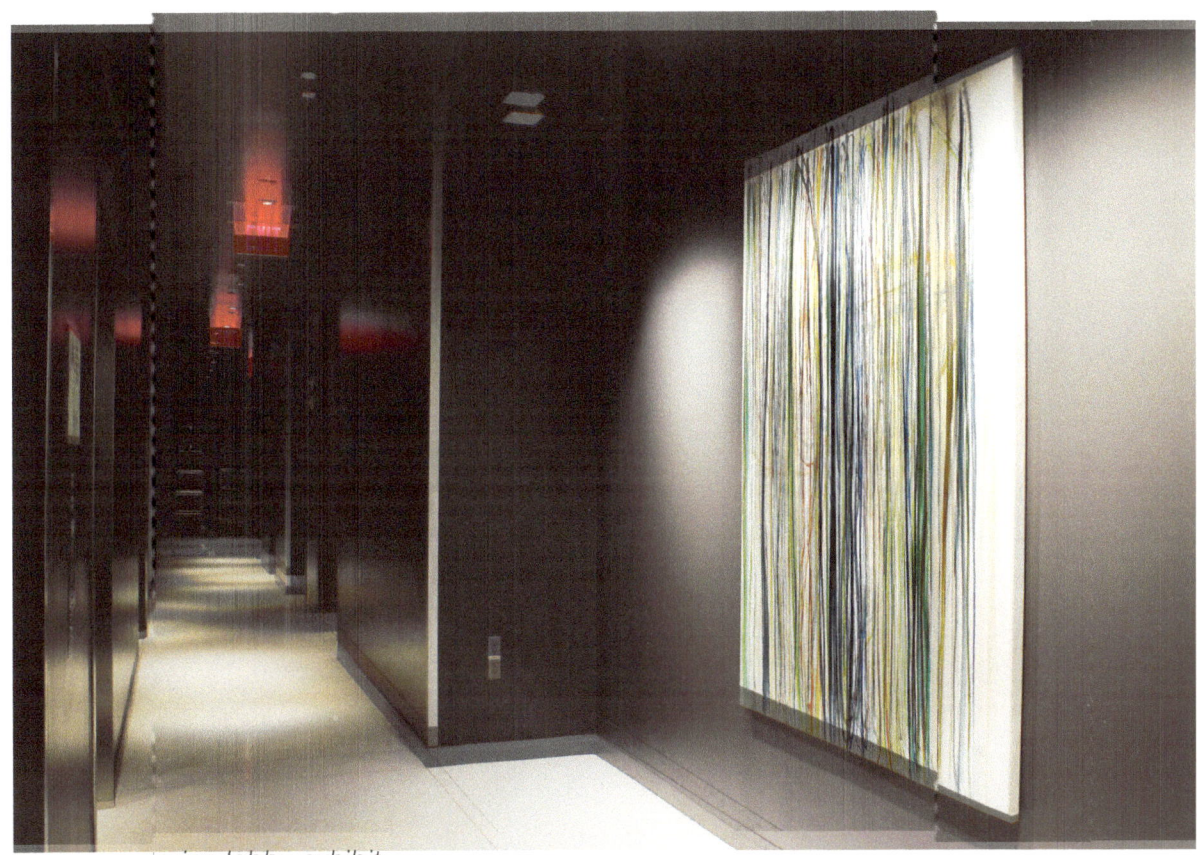

James Pustorino lobby exhibit

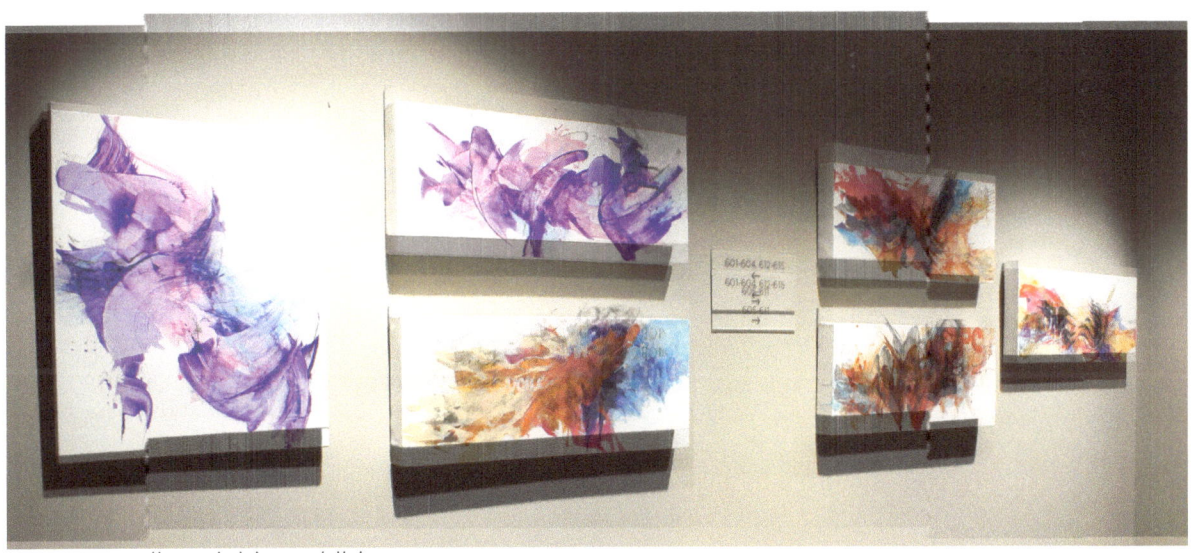

Bithika Adhikary lobby exhibit

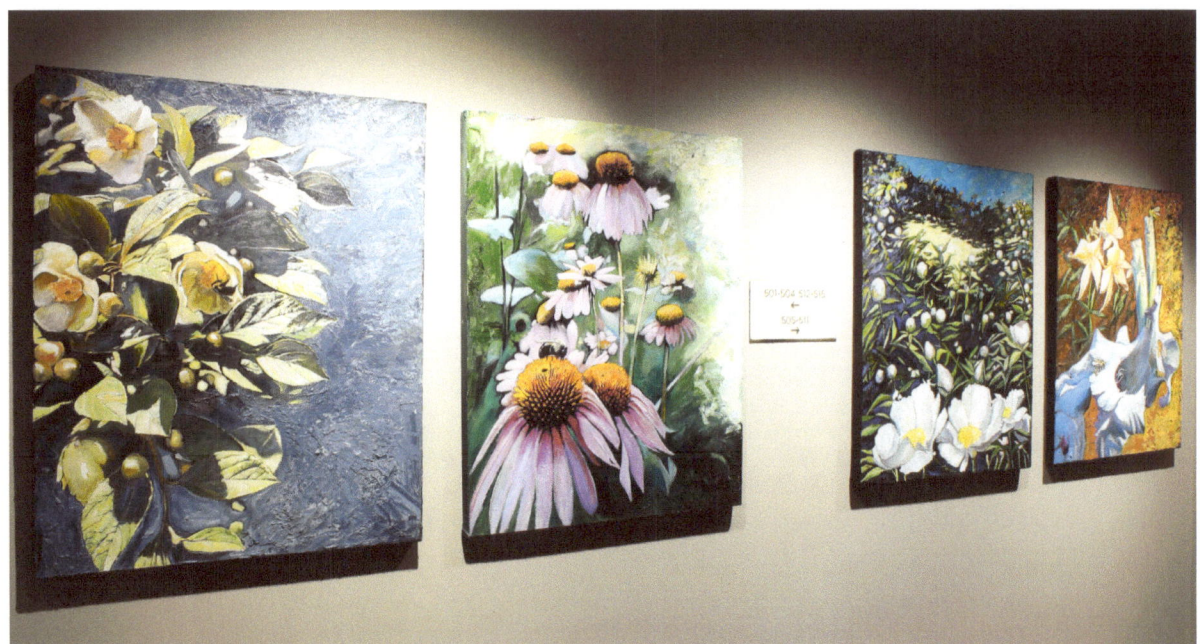
Peter Delman lobby exhibit

The Art House - 148 First St. Jersey City

Artists: Nan Ring, Stephen Krasner, Robert Egert, Alberte Bernier, Pauline Galiana, Aliza Augustine, Scot Wittman, Alan Walker, Roger Sayre, Tomomi Ono, Kate Dodd, and Glenn Garver.

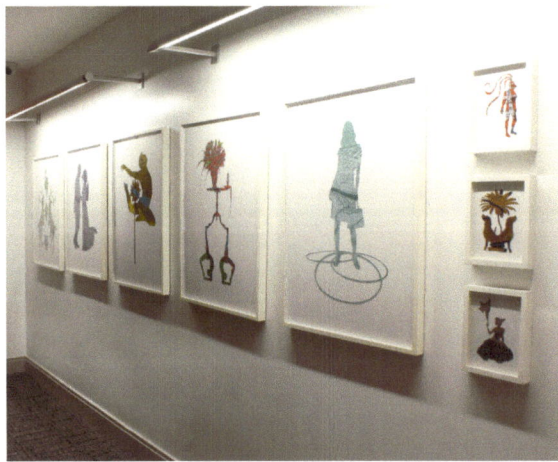
Scot Wittman lobby exhibit

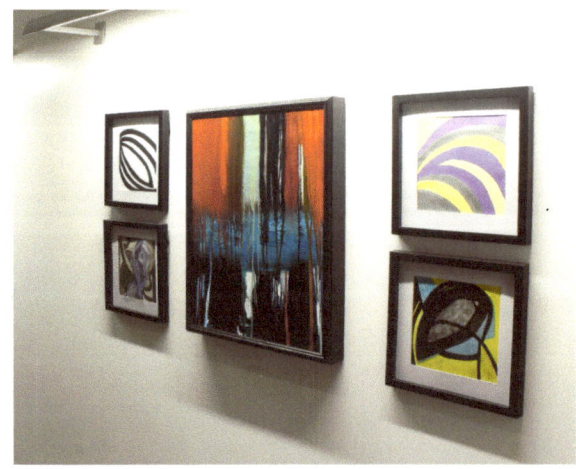
Alberte Bernier lobby exhibit

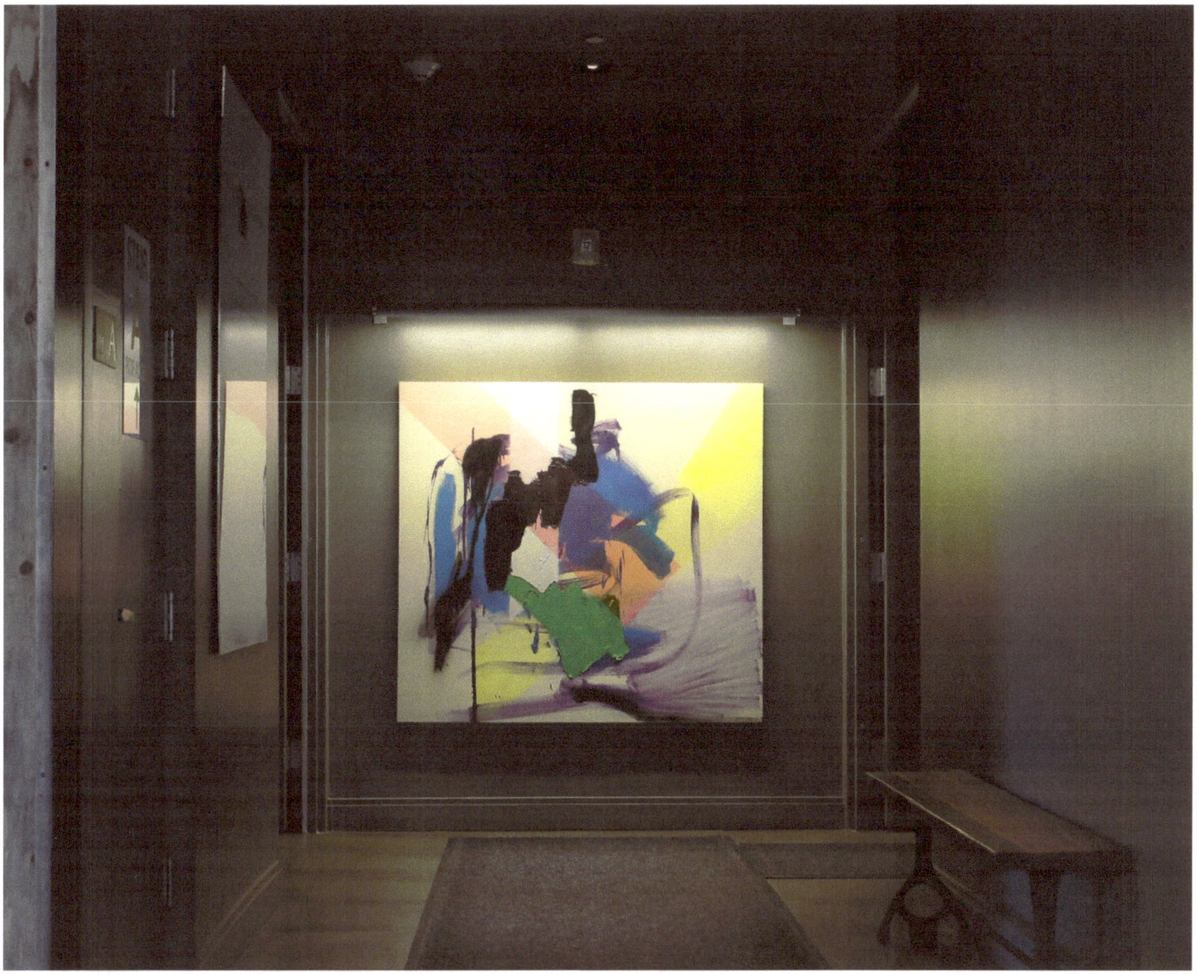

Glenn Garver, entrance lobby exhibit

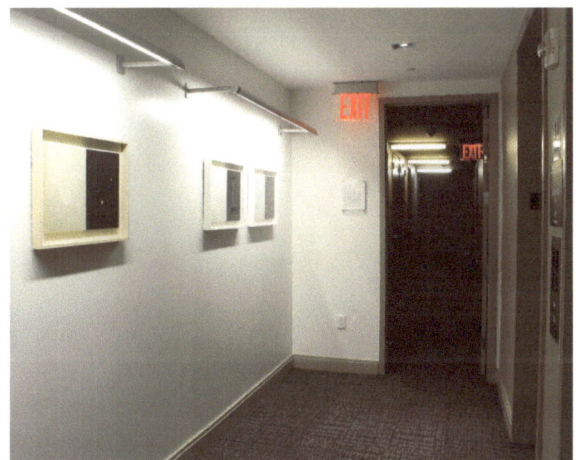

Tomomi Ono lobby exhibit

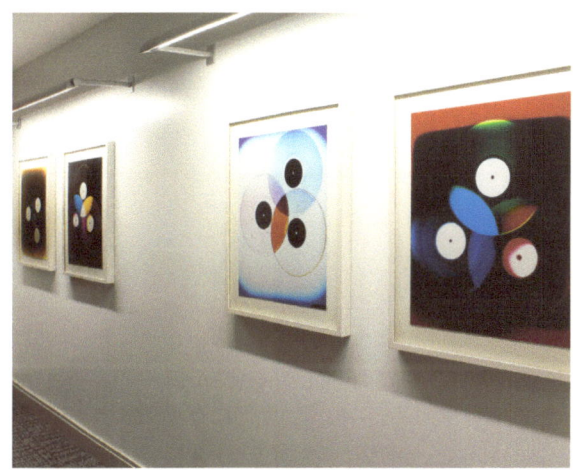

Roger Sayre lobby exhibit

Hamilton House - 255 Brunswick St. Jersey City

Artist: Matt Caulfield, Monika Kalra, Michael Endy, Deirdre Kennedy, Claire McConaughy, Bruce Halpin, Robert Streicher, and Jodie Fink.

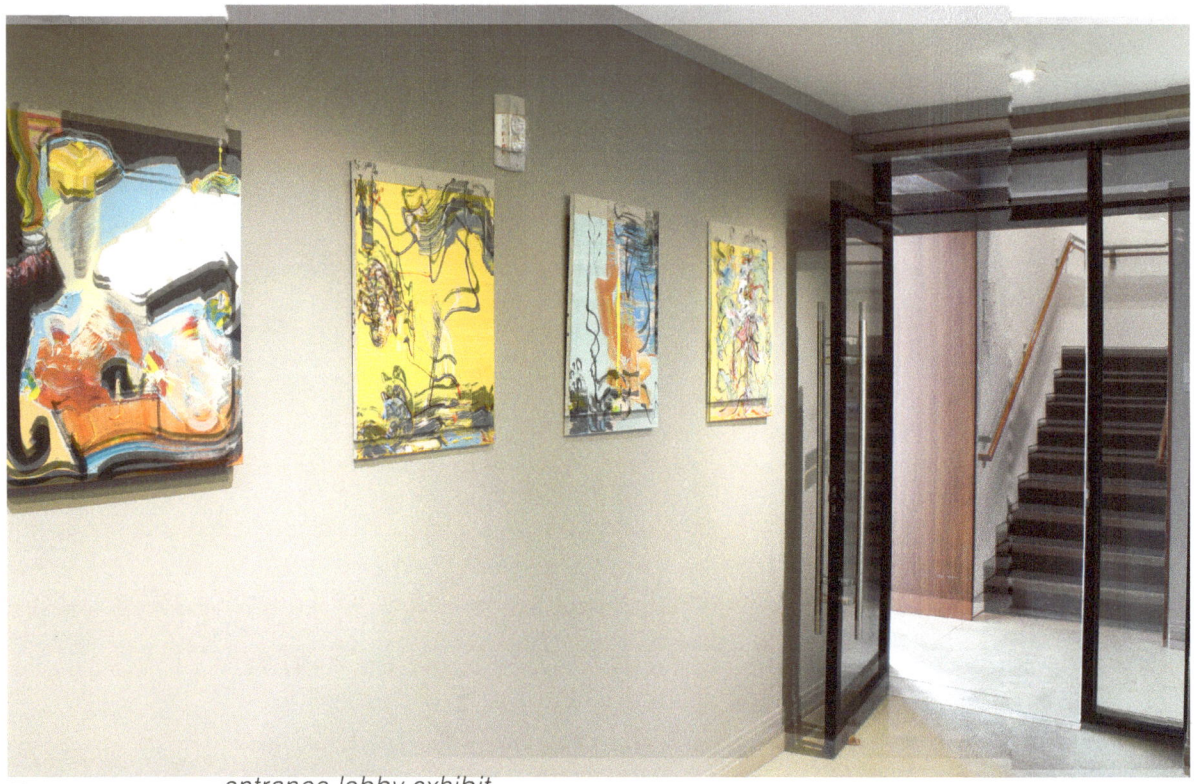

Robert Streicher, entrance lobby exhibit

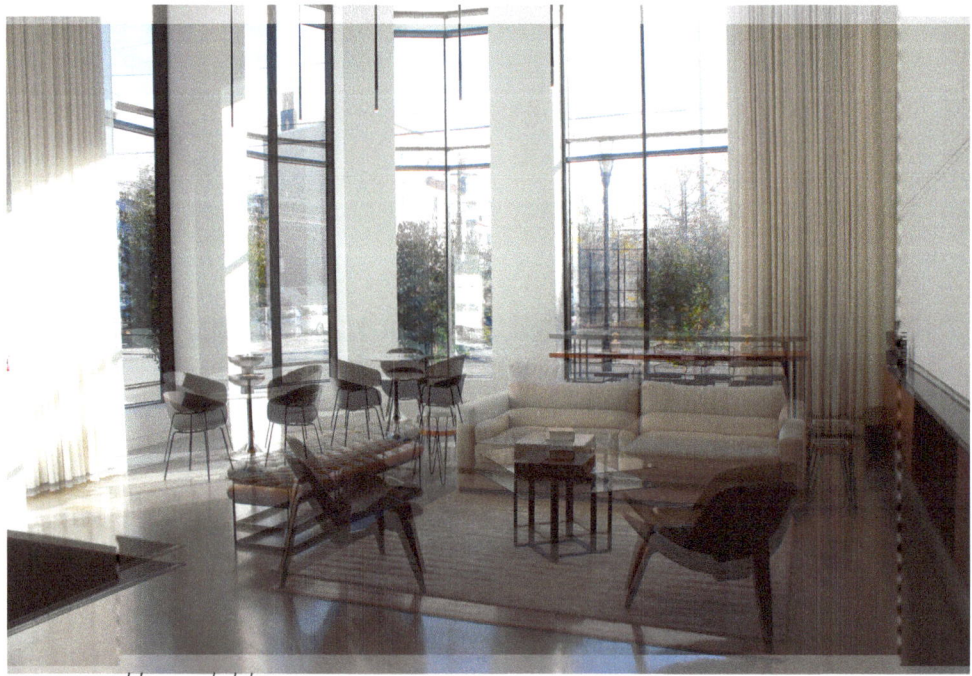

Hamilton House lobby area

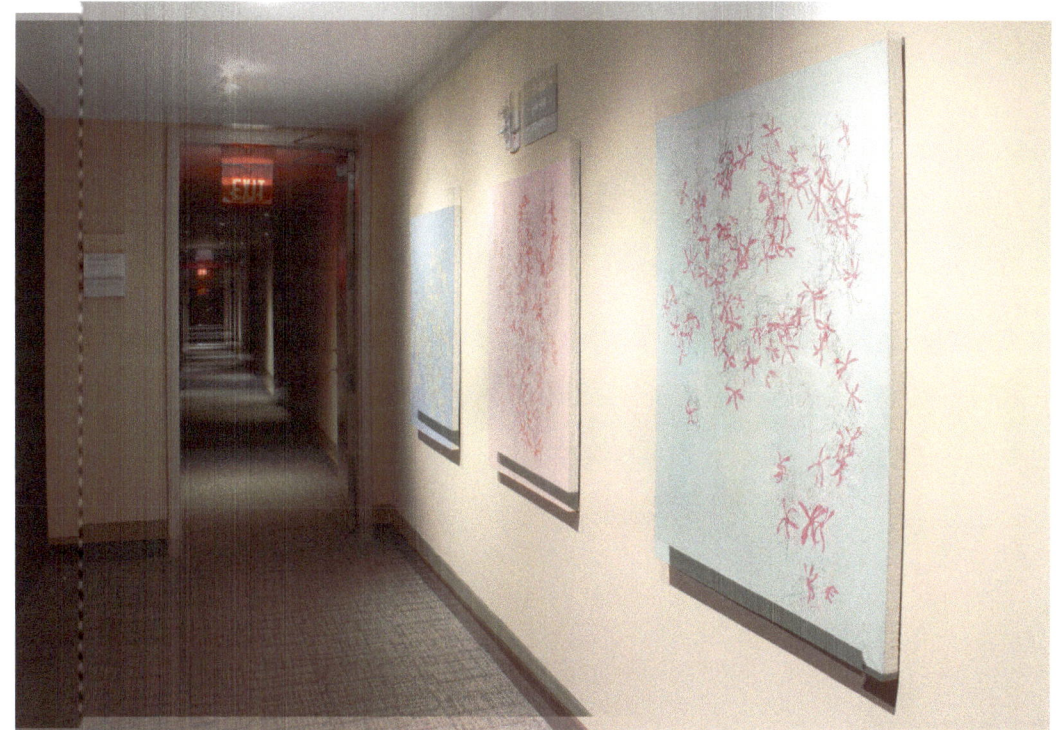

Claire McConaughy lobby exhibit

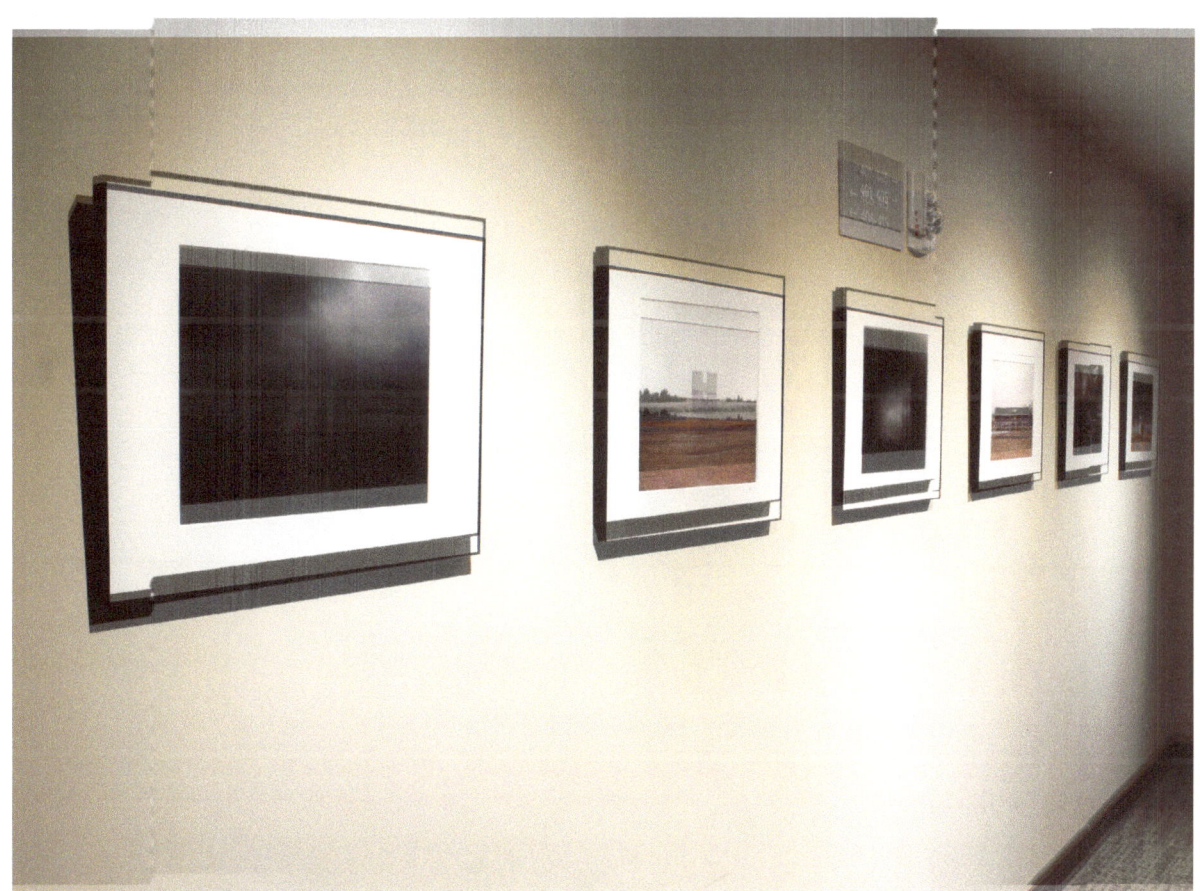

Michael Endy lobby exhibit

Rainbow Thursdays Artists

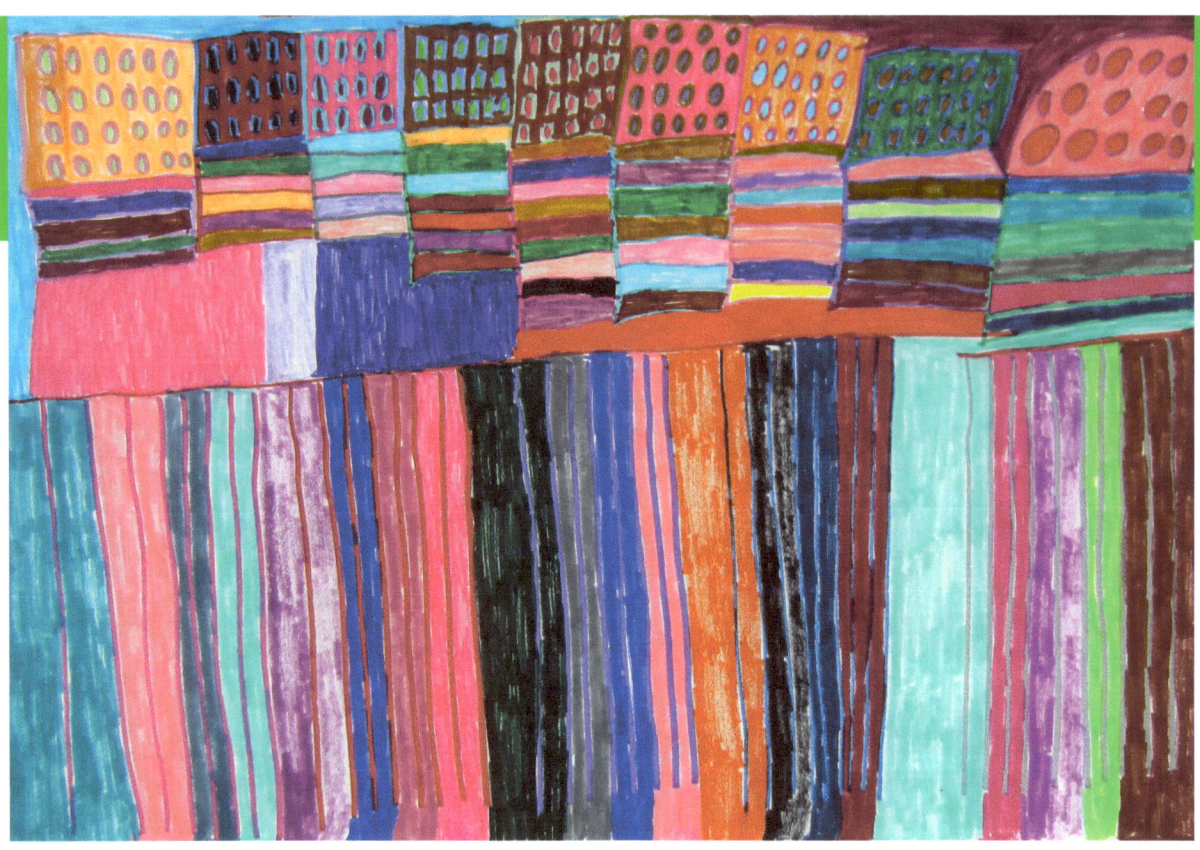

Drawing by Kaitlyn

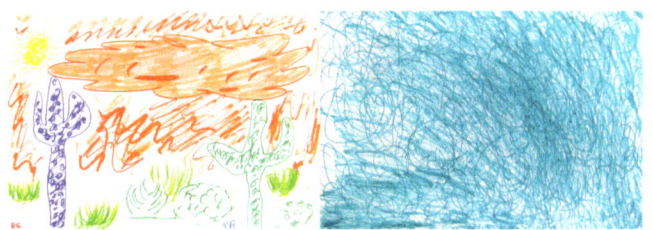
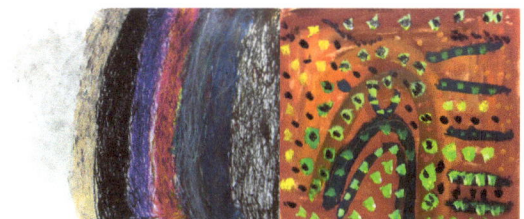

Victory Hall Inc.'s Rainbow Thursdays Artists Program continues to reach over 40 developmentally disabled adults each week in Bayonne and produce art exhibitions of the work to the public on a regular basis. This was our seventh season of programming at Windmill Center at 5th and Broadway, and in May, we started a second weekly program at Sunflower Center on Broadway in Bayonne.

We are scheduled to hold 90, 1.5 to 2hr classes per year serving over 40 adults with 3 to 5 artist/teachers and aids at each session.

Hundreds of pieces of artwork are produced each year and given as gifts and/or sold to family, friends and community members. The works express and communicate the talents of this population.

In 2018, the group's works were featured in a fundraiser event in conjunction with Windmill Center. From July-September 2018, we also held a 3 month-long exhibition at Bayonne Public Library and Windmill Center. Reports from family members of participants tell us that this program has made a real difference in the lives of our students, building motor skills, creativity, critical thinking, and giving them a new sense of accomplishment.

Although many of our participants continue to experience fragile health, the program continues to grow with new participants, and our early members are becoming very accomplished in their work.

Rainbow Thursdays Artists is a community-based art education program connecting disabled adults with professional artists who provide them with materials, training and encouragement to express themselves through art.

The program encompasses study of great artworks, the natural world, and images of people through books and photographs, and encourages each participant to understand drawing as their unique visual language with which they can create realistic and abstract form and systems, and express emotion and ideas through line and color.

The opportunity to exhibit and sell their artwork to family, friends and many supporters in the community allows Rainbow Thursdays Artists to become visible and valued in a new way.

Program Manager and Lead Teacher is **Jill Scipione**.

Teachers are artists **James Pustorino**, and **Bruno Nadalin**.

Rainbow Thursdays Artists classes are presented free of charge, and are funded in part by a CDBG grant from the City of Bayonne and a Provident Foundation Grant for 2018.

If you would like to learn more about our program, please contact us at ou email address: **info@drawingrooms.org**

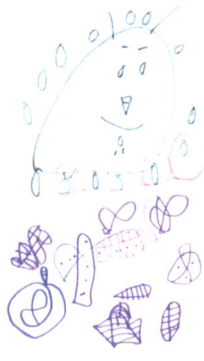

Sunflower Adult Medical Day Care Center, Bayonne, NJ

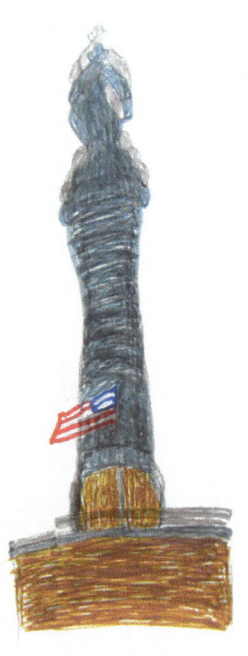
Maryann Liberty Monument

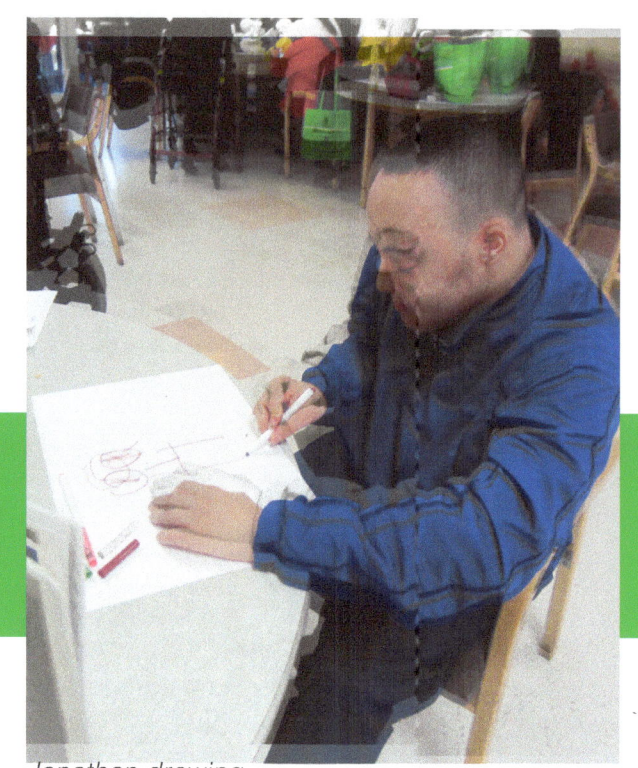
Jonathan drawing

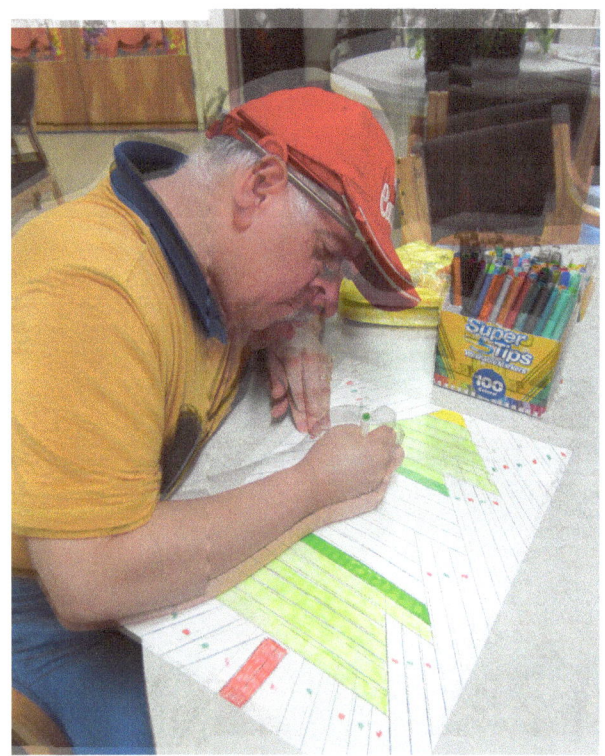
Ramone drawing

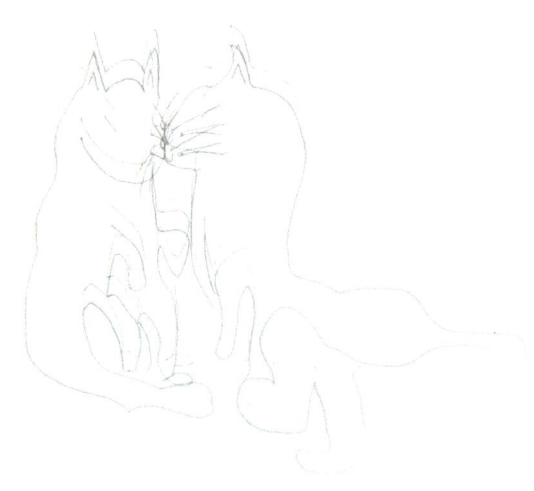
Cats by Heather

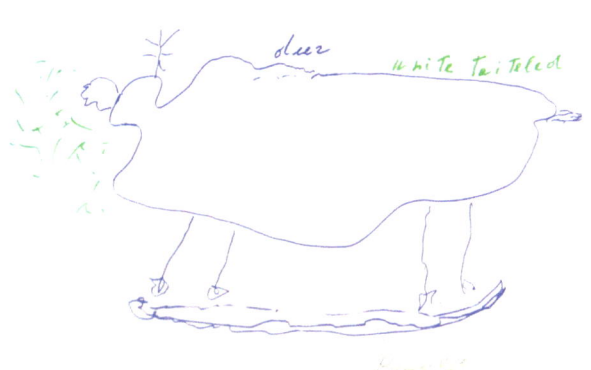

White Tailed Deer by Giuseppe

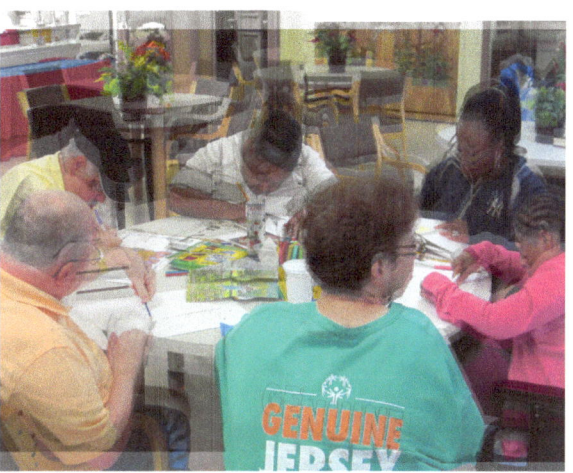

Sunflower group drawing

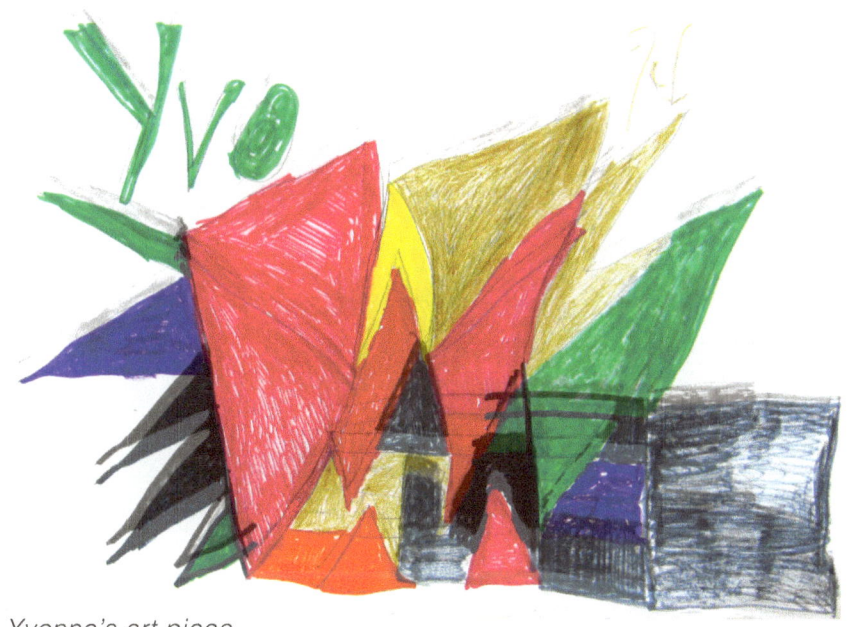

Yvonne's art piece

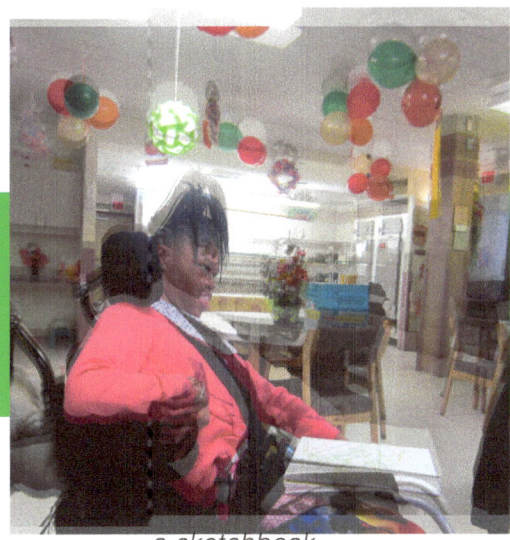

Raven with a sketchbook

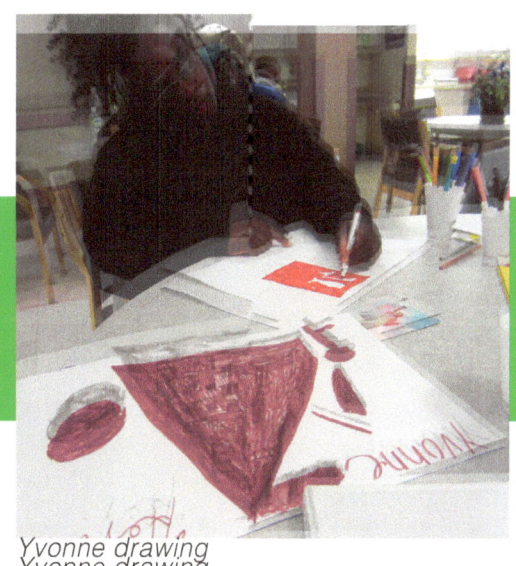

Yvonne drawing

47 Rainbow Thursdays

Windmill Center, Bayonne, NJ

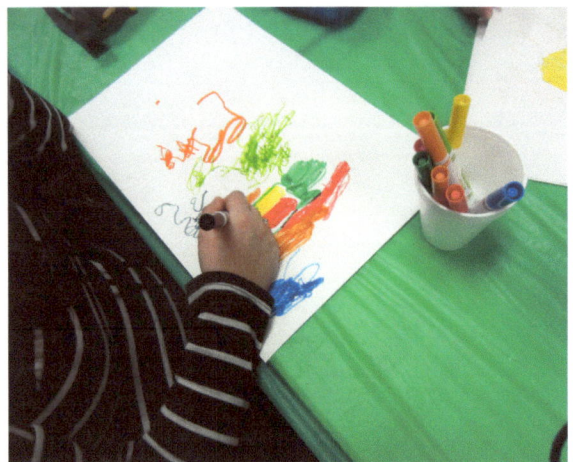
Wendy drawing

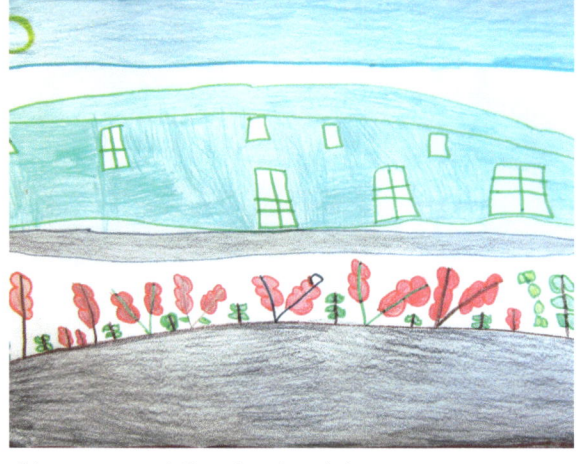
Chateau and Garden by Johnny

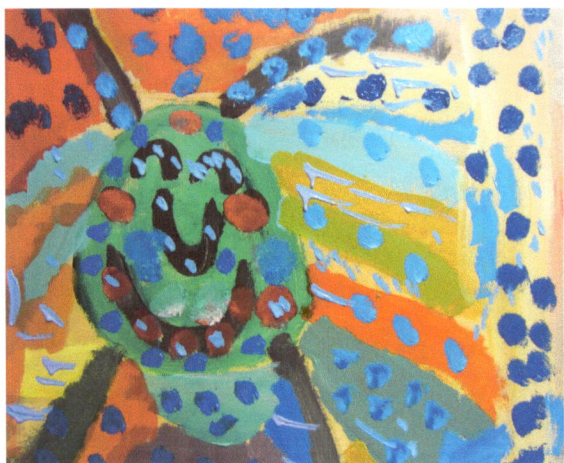
Wayne's art piece

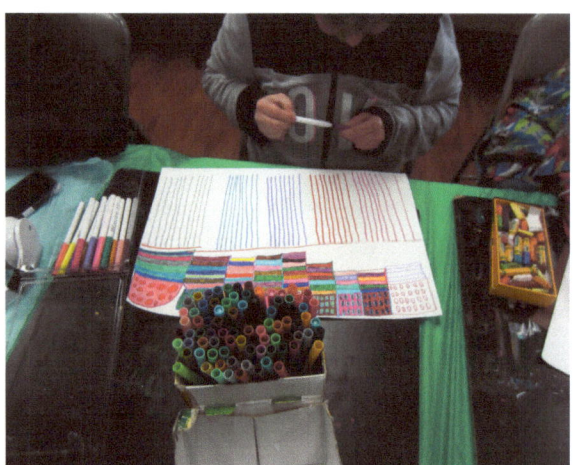
Kaitlyn drawing

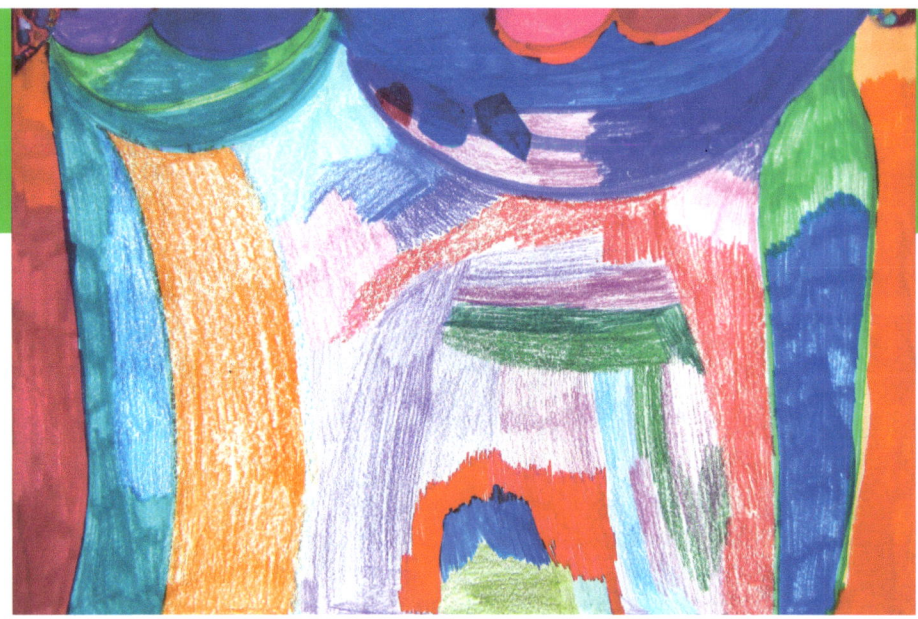
Curtains by Yahira

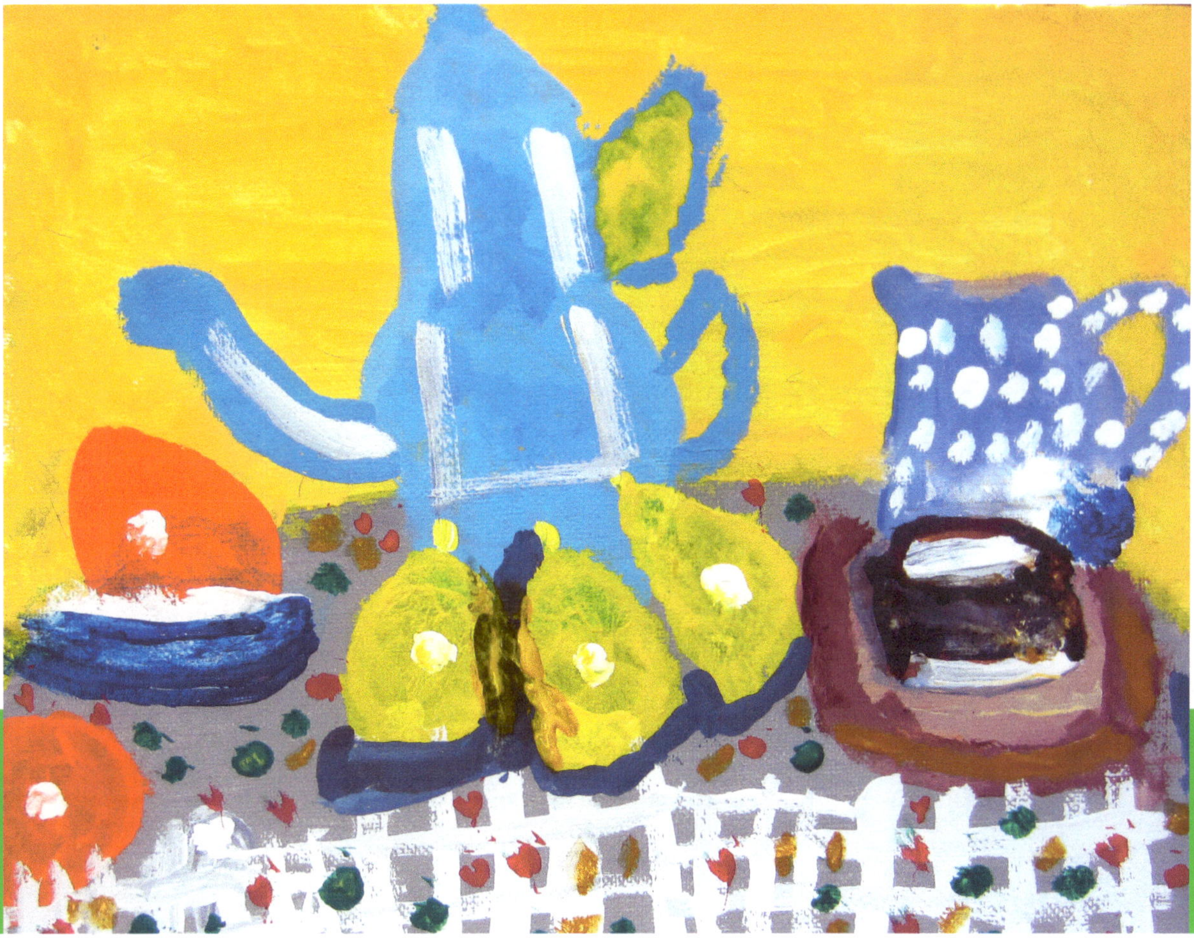

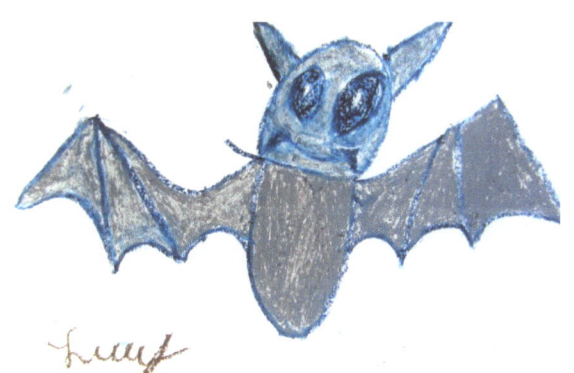

Timothy's still life after Van Gogh

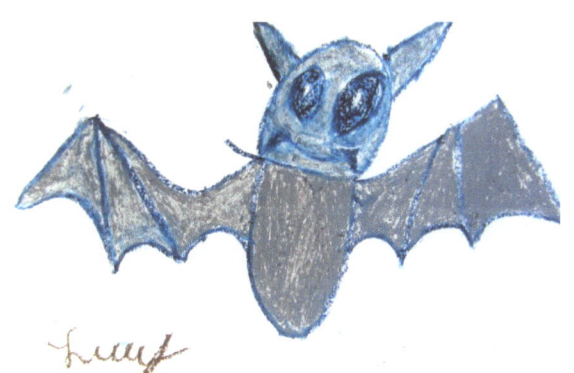

Bat by Luis B

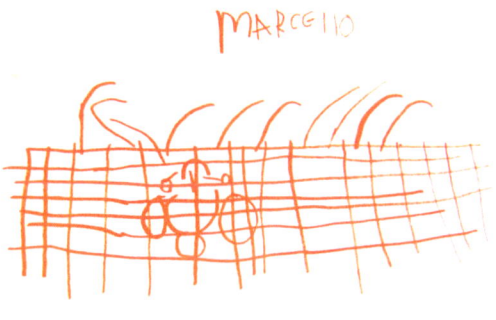

Marcello's art piece

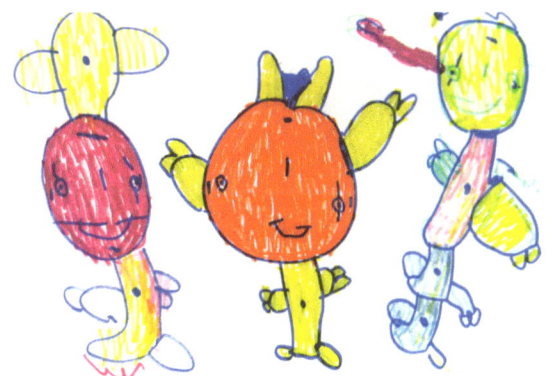

Happy Shmoos by Mary Beth

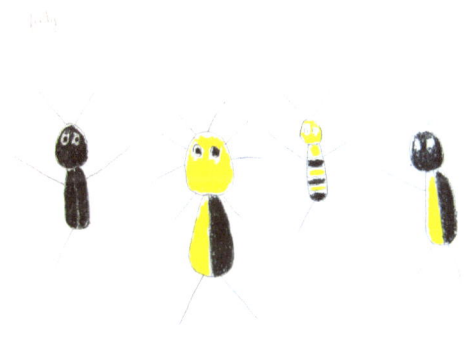

Beetles by Judy

VICTORY HALL INC. MAJOR SPONSORS AND SUPPORTERS 2018-19

The Geraldine R. Dodge Foundation
Qualcomm
City of Bayonne, CDBG
Hudson County LAP
Mario and Anna Scipione
Kay Cook and Perry Pogany
Forest City Realty
Provident Bank

VICTORY HALL INC. STAFF

Executive Director: James Pustorino
Exhibitions Director / Curator: Anne Trauben:
Program Manager, Rainbow Thursdays Artists: Jill Scipione
Teaching Artist: Bruno Nadalin, and James Pustorino
Interns: Alejandro Rubin, and Denise Cateron

BOARD MEMBERS

President: Daniel Frohwirth
Vice President: Danielle Brooks
Secretary: John B. ("Jack") Starr, Jr., Ph.D., and Bruce Halpin
Treasurer: Paul Dennison

COMMITTEE MEMBERS

Shazzi Thomas
Mona Brody

THANKS to all who consulted and assisted us in our BUILD-OUT and MOVE!
Kenneth Foreman, Tim Heins, Richard Garber/GRO Architects, David French, Christo Pratt, Edward Fausty, Richard White, Dan Volker, and Dwayne Gayle

THANKS TO OUR DONORS AND SPONSORS!

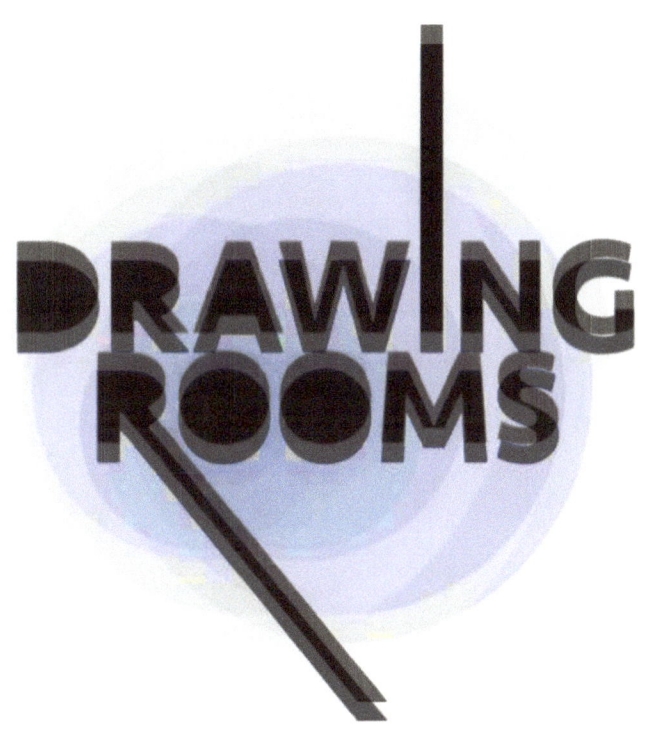

Thank You for your commitment to the Arts!
Providing excellent programming in your innovative gallery for Jersey City artists is the greatest VICTORY of all!

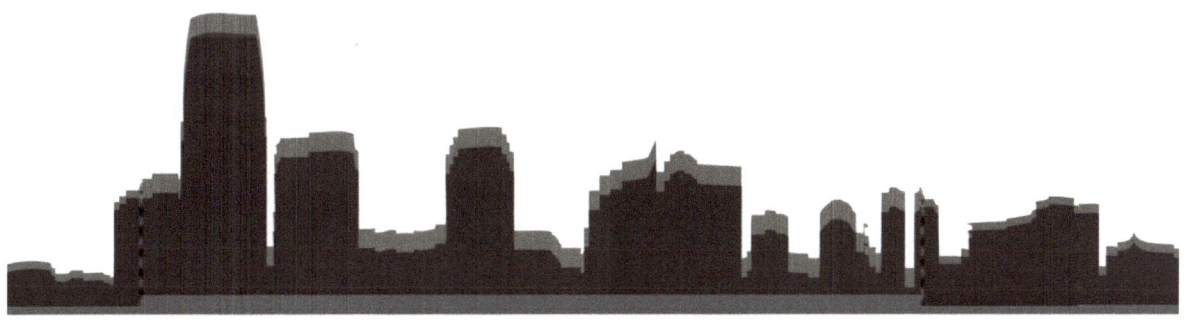

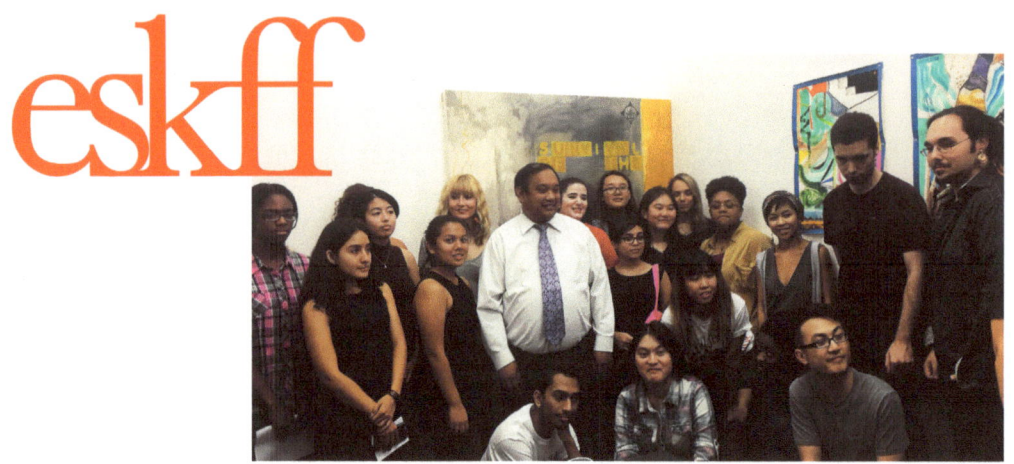

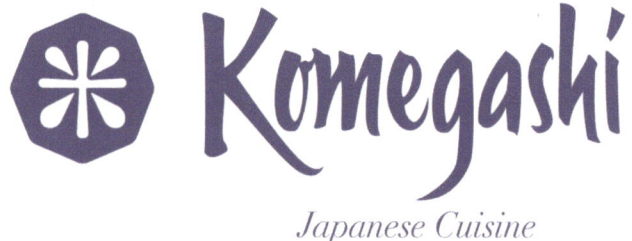

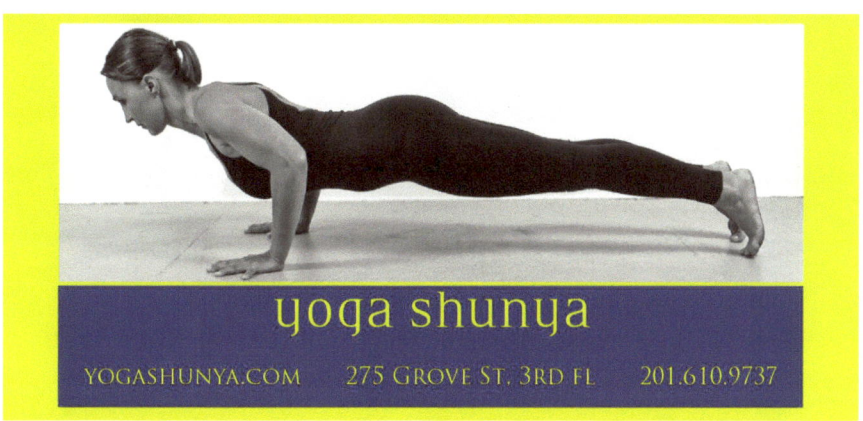

OKOKOSTUDIO

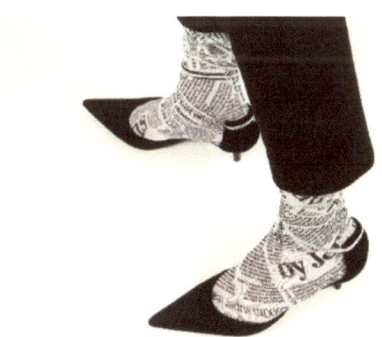

www.okokostudio.com

Congratulates Drawing Rooms on this Exciting Step!

www.ingramcontent.com/pod-product-compliance
Lightning Source LLC
Chambersburg PA
CBHW051924210526
45473CB00006B/2126